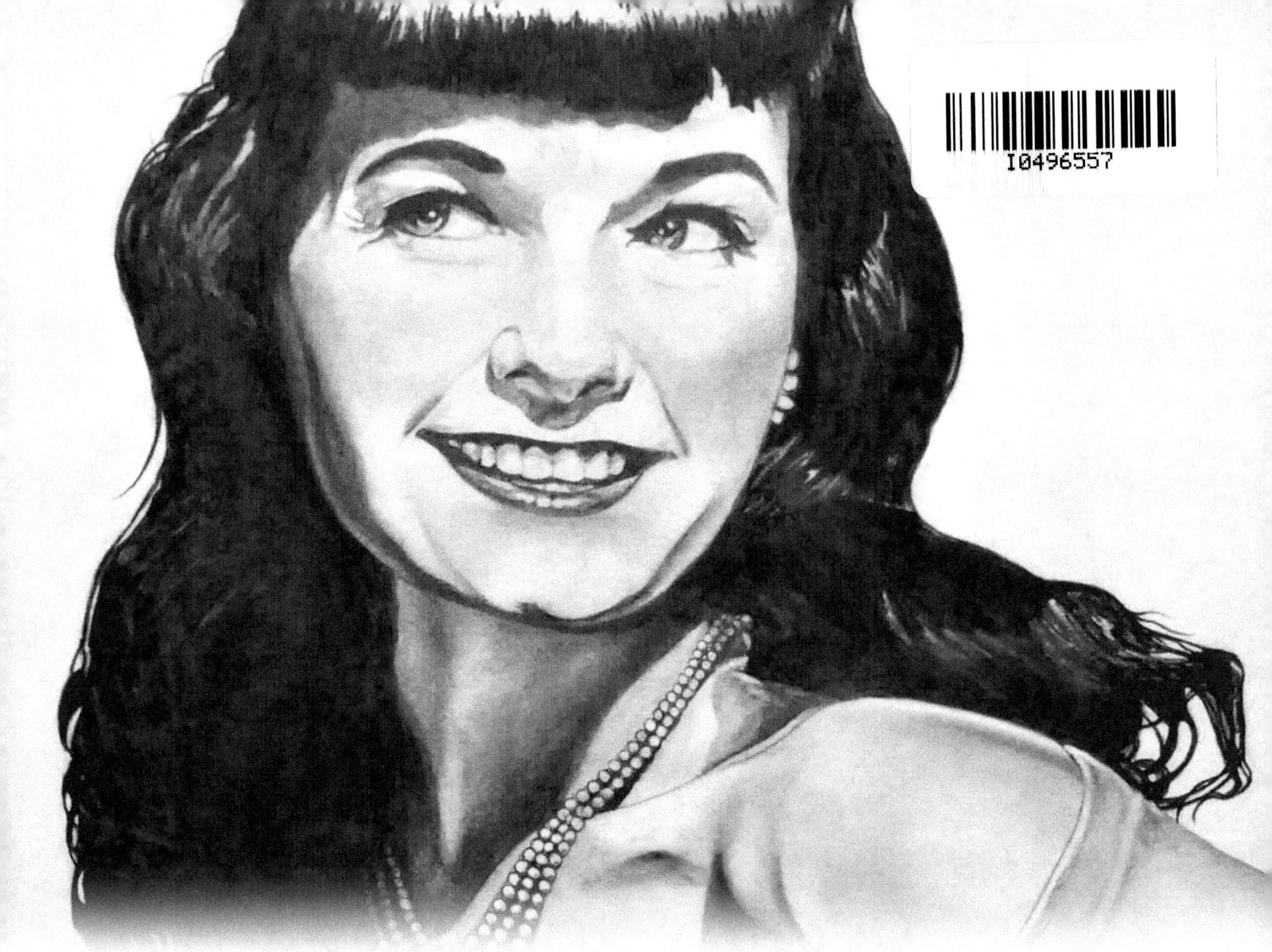

ARTWORK BY **BILL POLICY**
EDITED AND DESIGNED BY **CARISSA PARDEE**

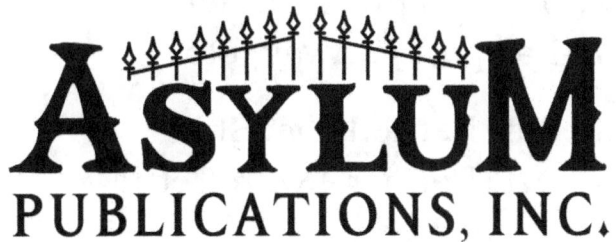

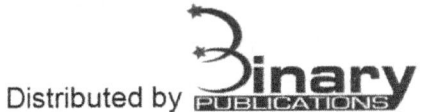

CEO AND EDITOR IN CHIEF **PAUL BURKE**
CREATIVE DIRECTOR **JOSHUA WERNER**

ISBN: 978-1-7363197-3-4

Bettie Page: The Queen of Pinups™. Published by Asylum Publications, Inc. ™ © by Bill Policy. Asylum Publications, Inc. logo TM 2023. All rights reserved. No portion of this publication may be reproduced or transmitted, in any form by any means, without written consent from the Publisher, except for any small excerpts for the purpose of review. For further information regarding custom photo/art books, ordering wholesale, or other inquiries, please write to asylumpublications75@gmail.com.

www.asylumpublications.com

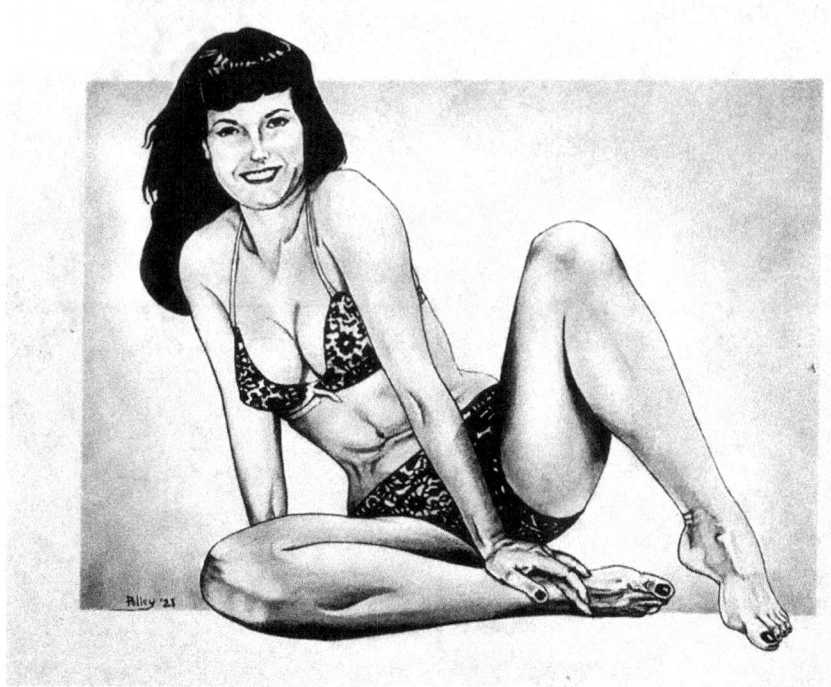

Bettie Page

Queen of the Pinups

In 2018 I started a pinup series called "the Maidens of Moosepuke" (after my studio). It is an irreverent look at the pinup genre. Some examples include a beautiful young woman sitting atop a stack of pancakes, a 300 foot tall woman perched on the Eiffel Tower, a model reclining on an international airport runway, etc.

It was during this time I became interested in Bettie Page. She was perfectly suited for my drawing "Scenic Mt. Rainier", with Bettie standing, one knee resting atop the Seattle Space Needle.

In my search for pinup poses I began to encounter more and more images of Bettie, so I began to investigate this alluring beauty.

Copyright   2022 Bill Policy. All rights reserved. Edited by Carissa Pardee.

Some say that the camera loved Bettie. Indeed, but Bettie loved it right back. Yes, she had that "girl next door" look. She could also be submissive, or sultry, or whatever the situation called for. She loved to model, and as she once said, "It beats pounding on a typewriter for 8 hours a day."

Thousands of photos were taken of Bettie, and her legacy as the Queen of Pinups will never fade.

In Bettie's case I abandoned my "irreverent" approach to the pinup. Bettie is the perfect pinup just the way she is.

Bill Policy

Moosepuke Studio

Denver CO USA

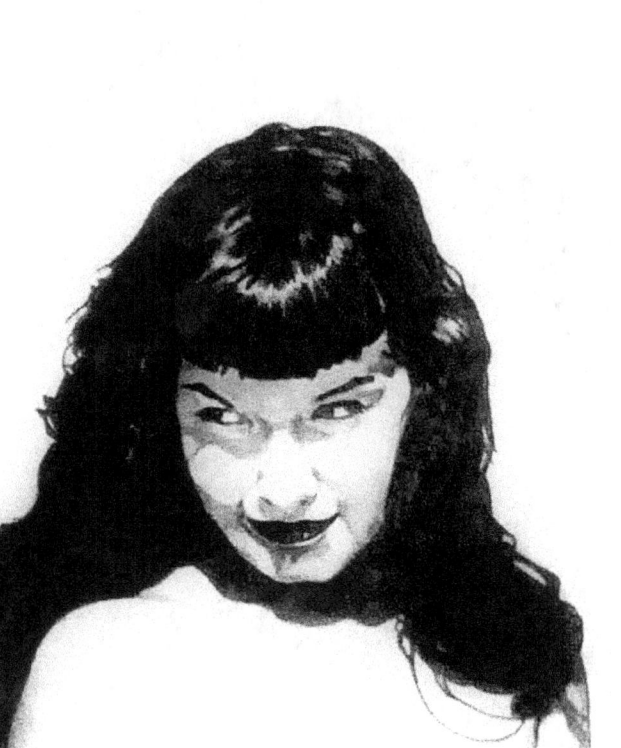

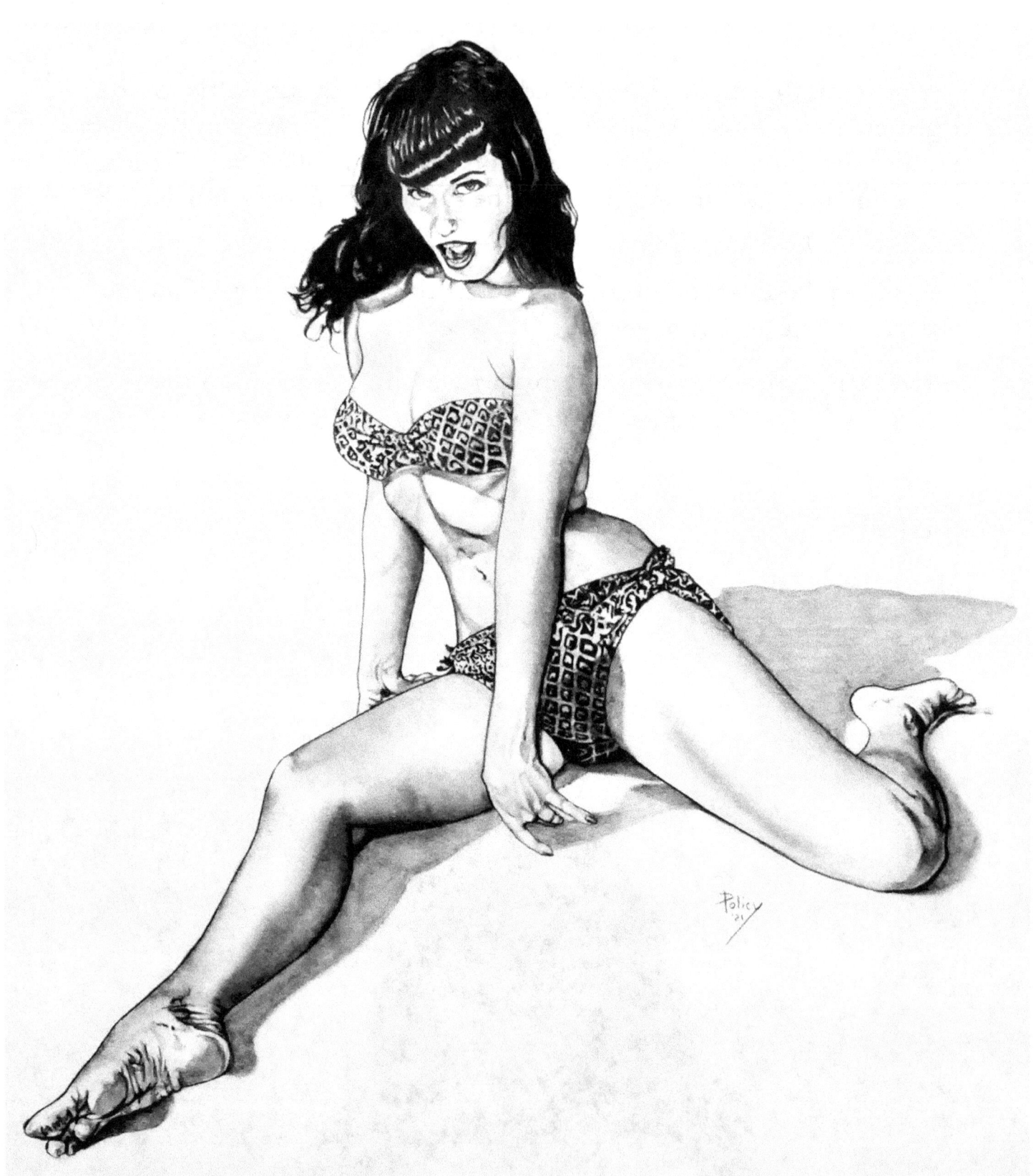

Bathing Beauty

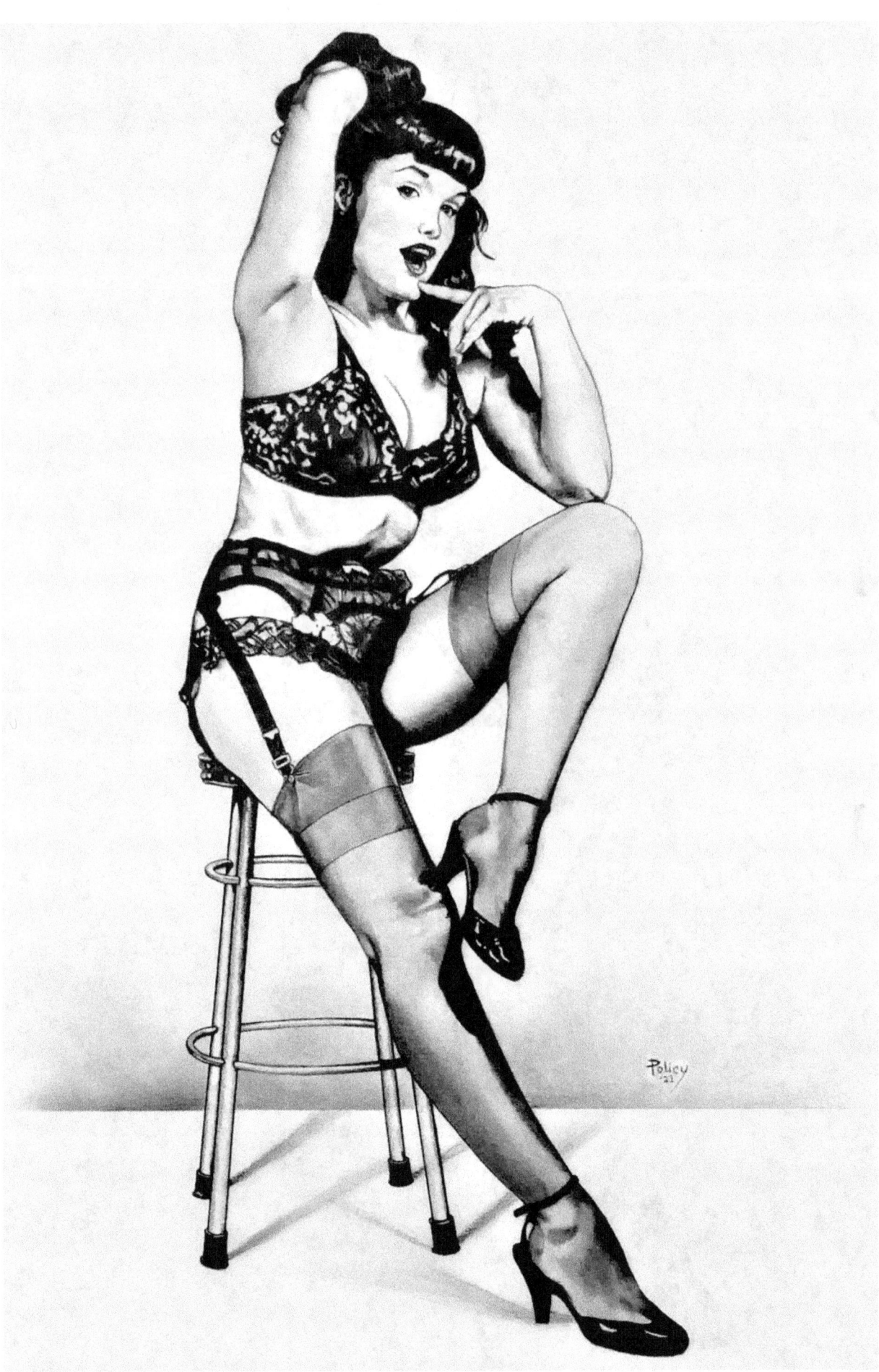

Lucky Stool

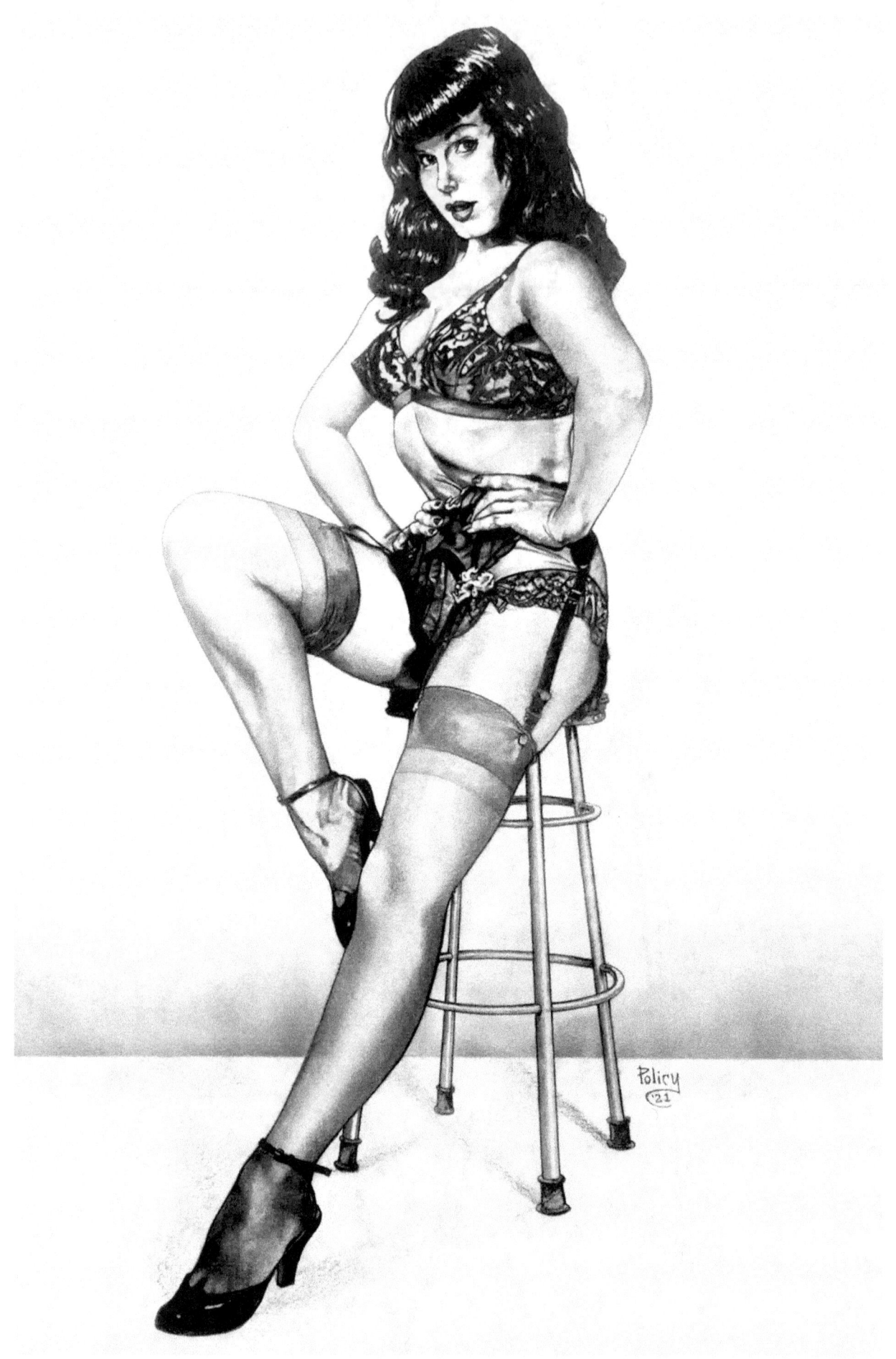

Just Checking

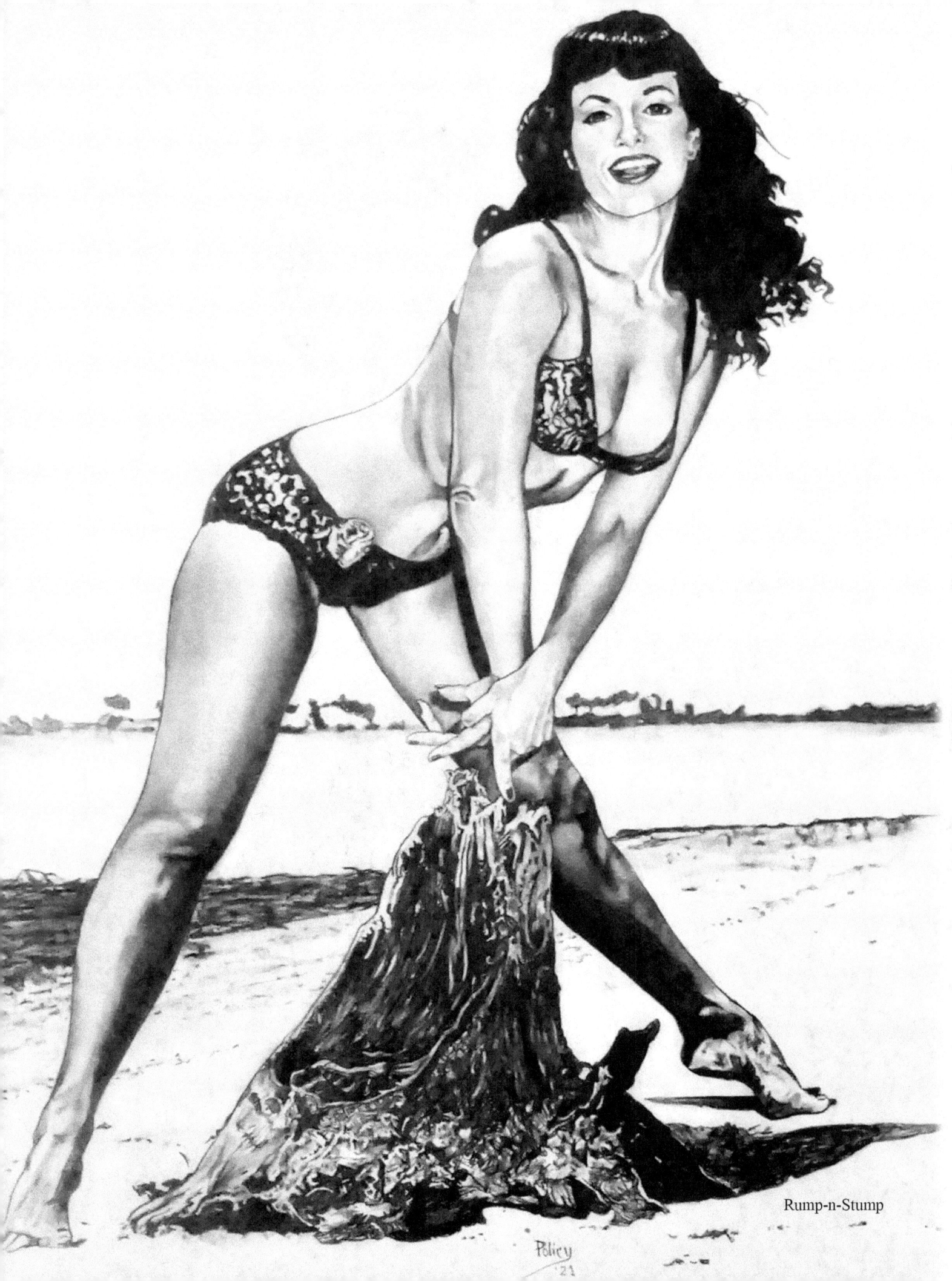
Rump-n-Stump

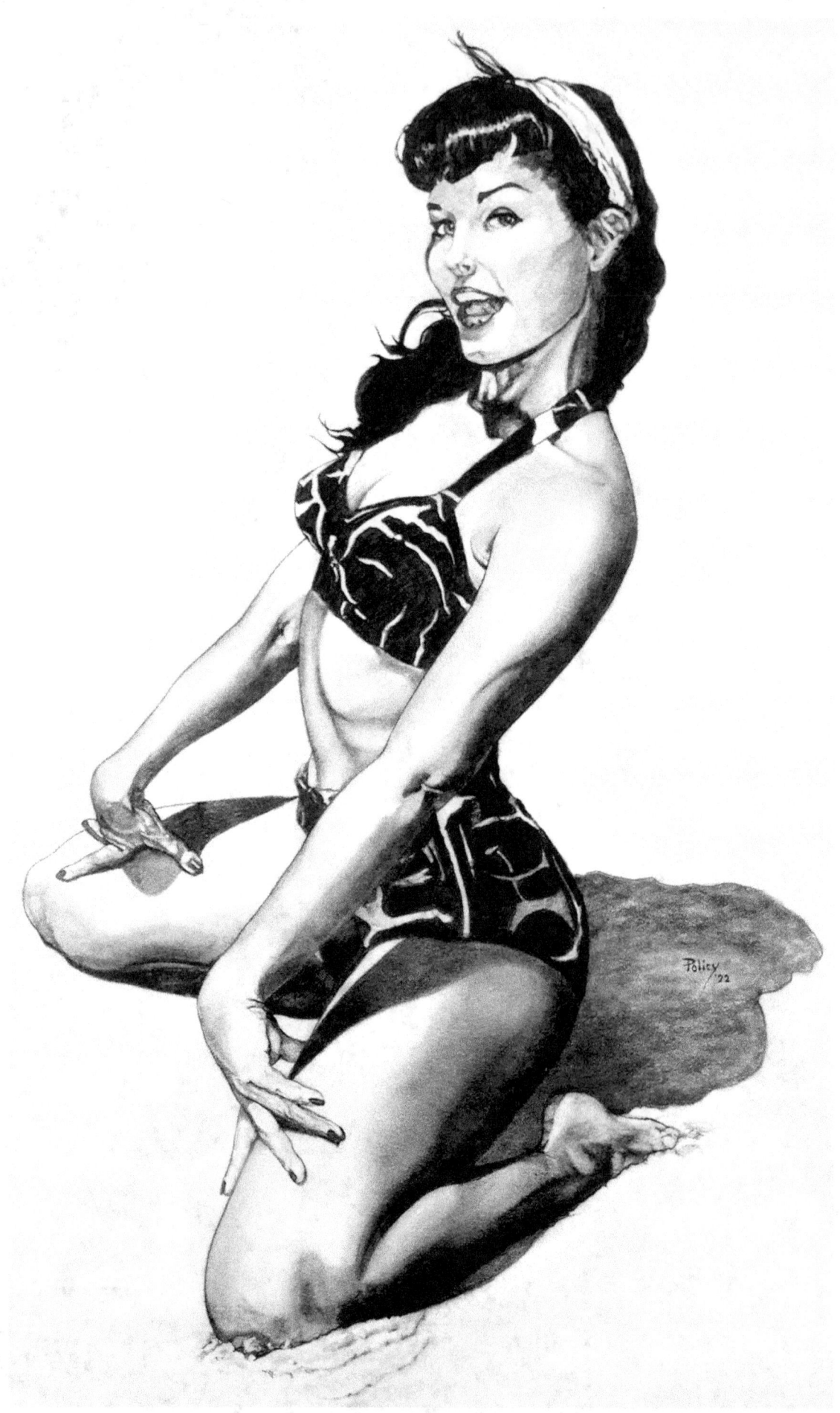

Hi!

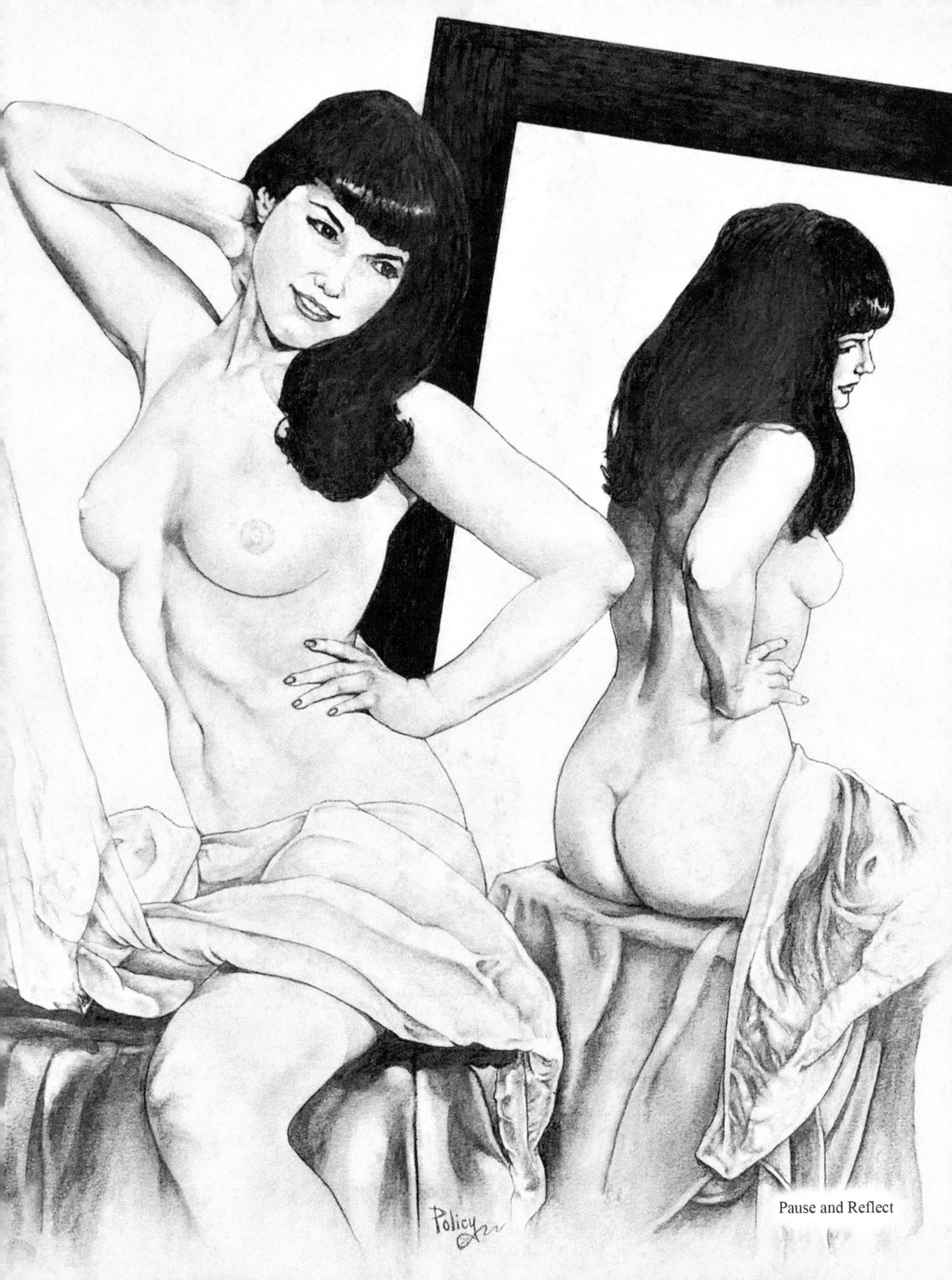

Pause and Reflect

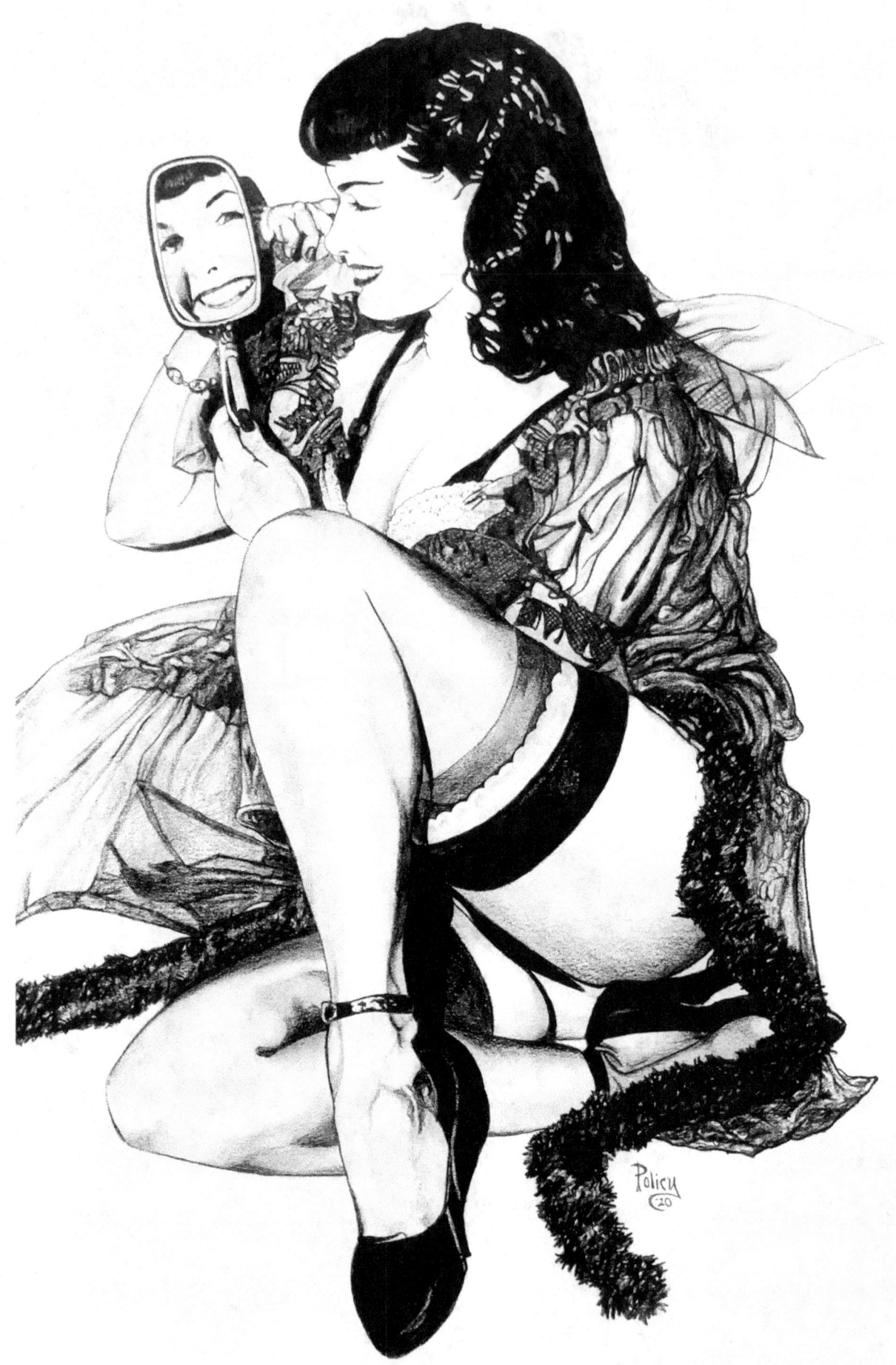

Peek-A-Boo

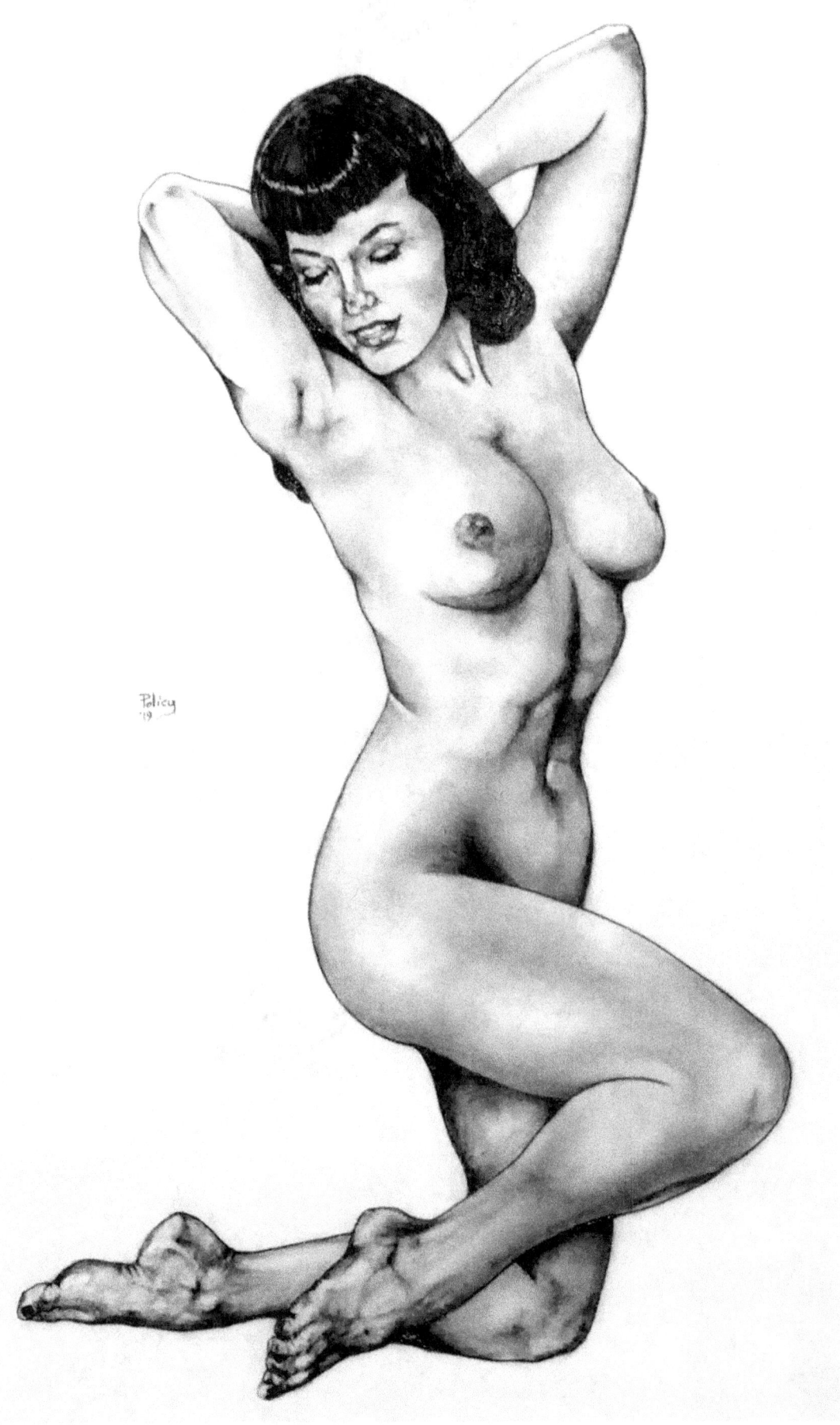

Daydream

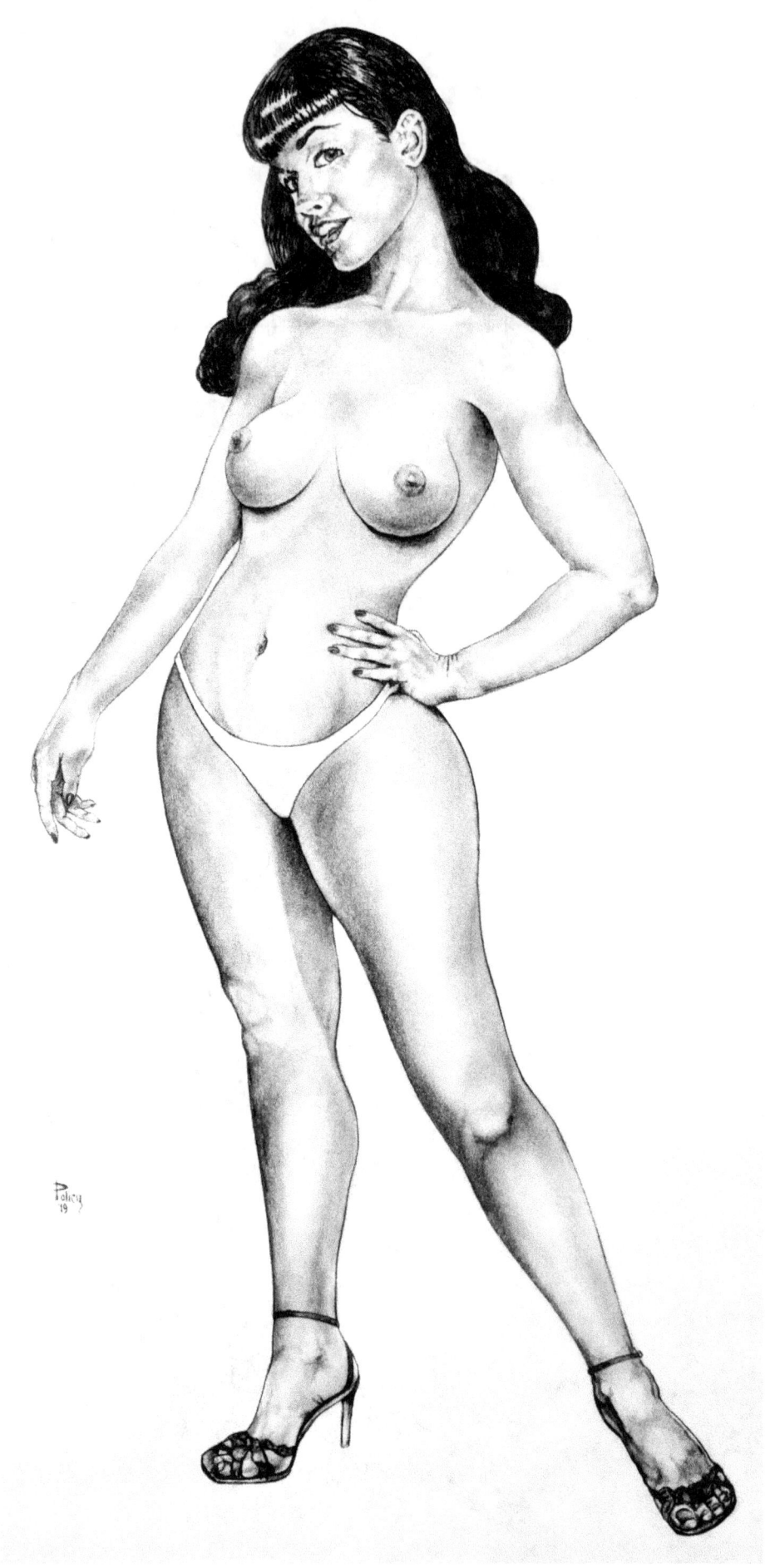

So There

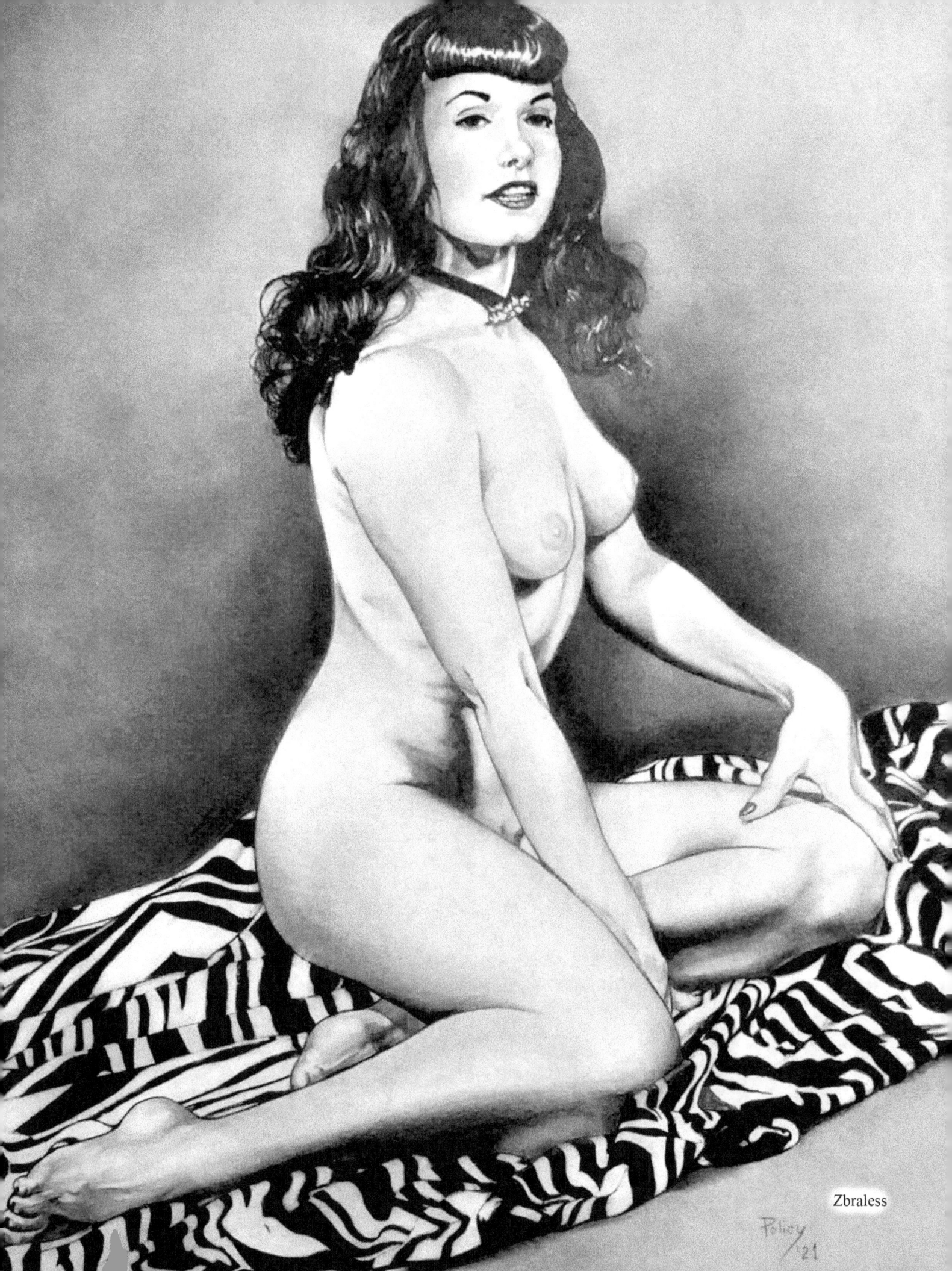

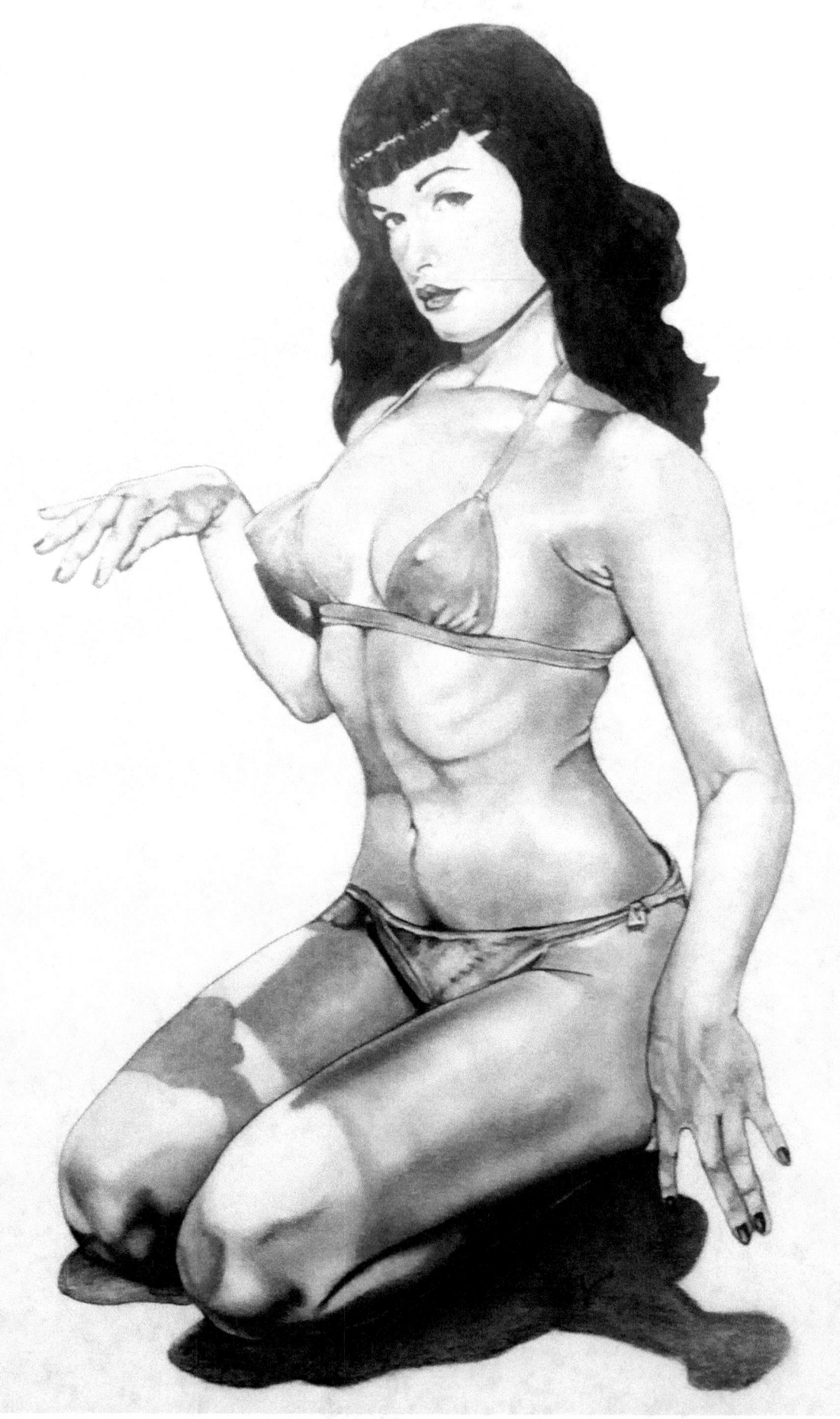

Like What You See

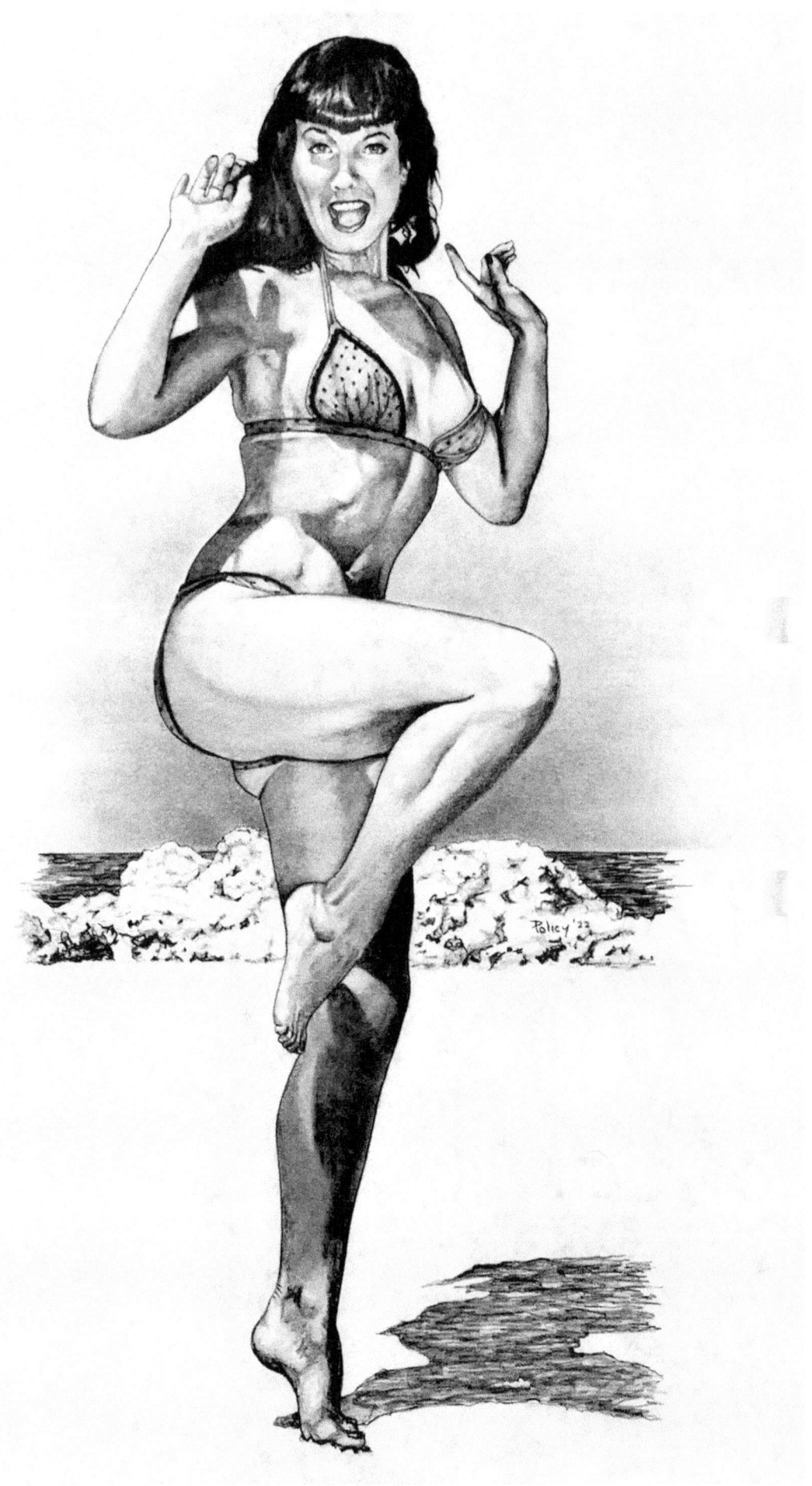

Best Blue Bikini

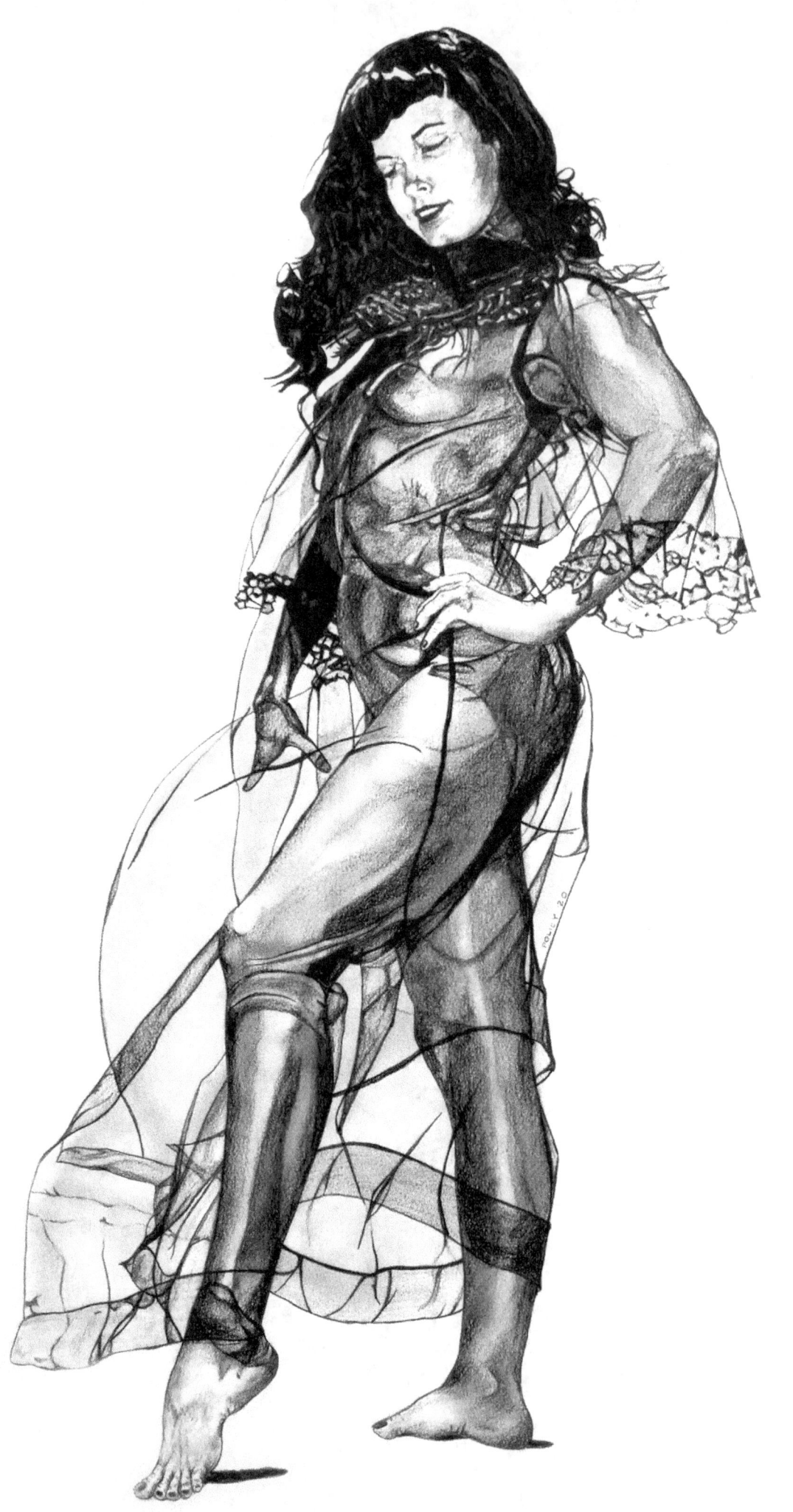

Aerie

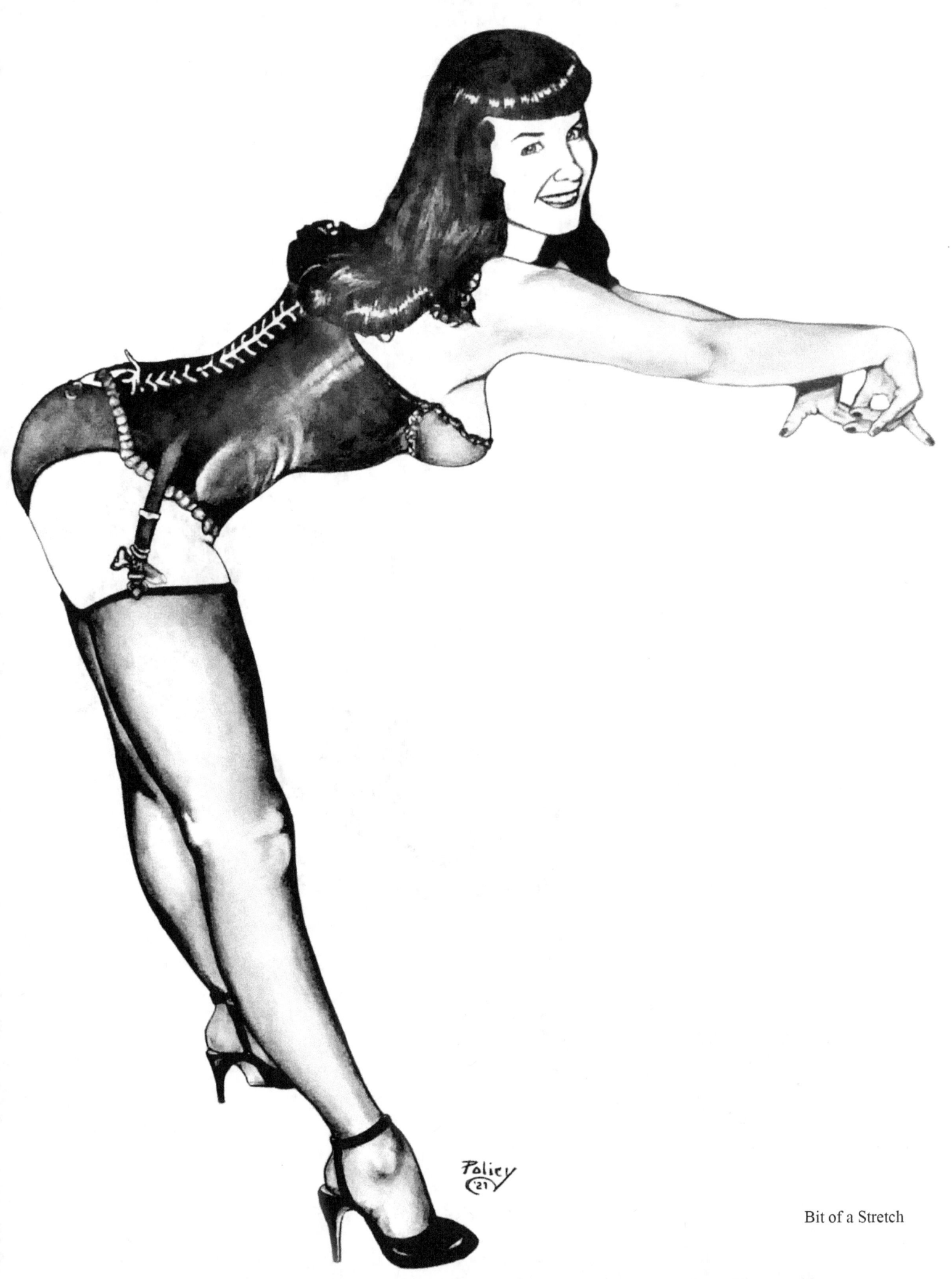

Bit of a Stretch

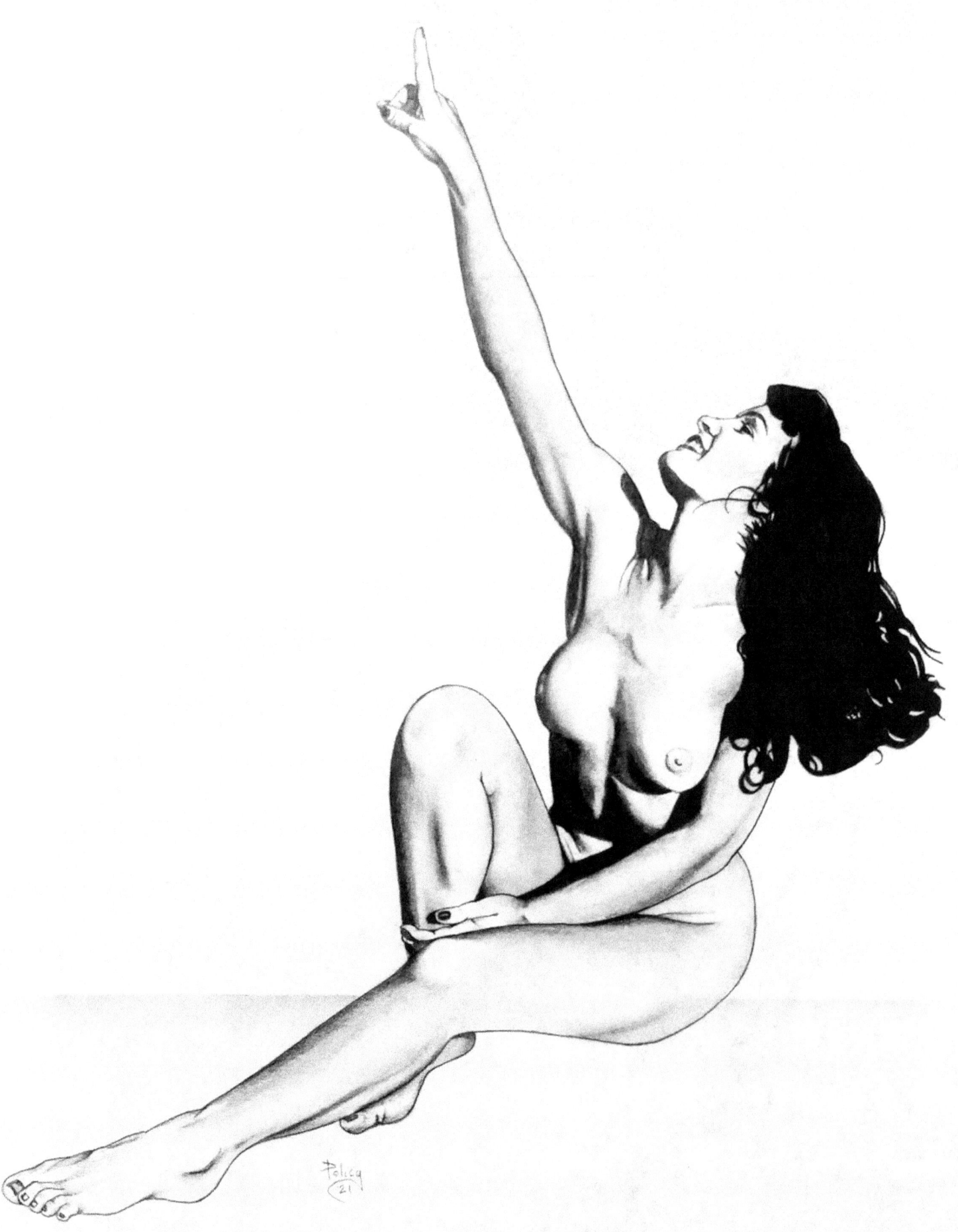

It's a Bird, It's a Plane

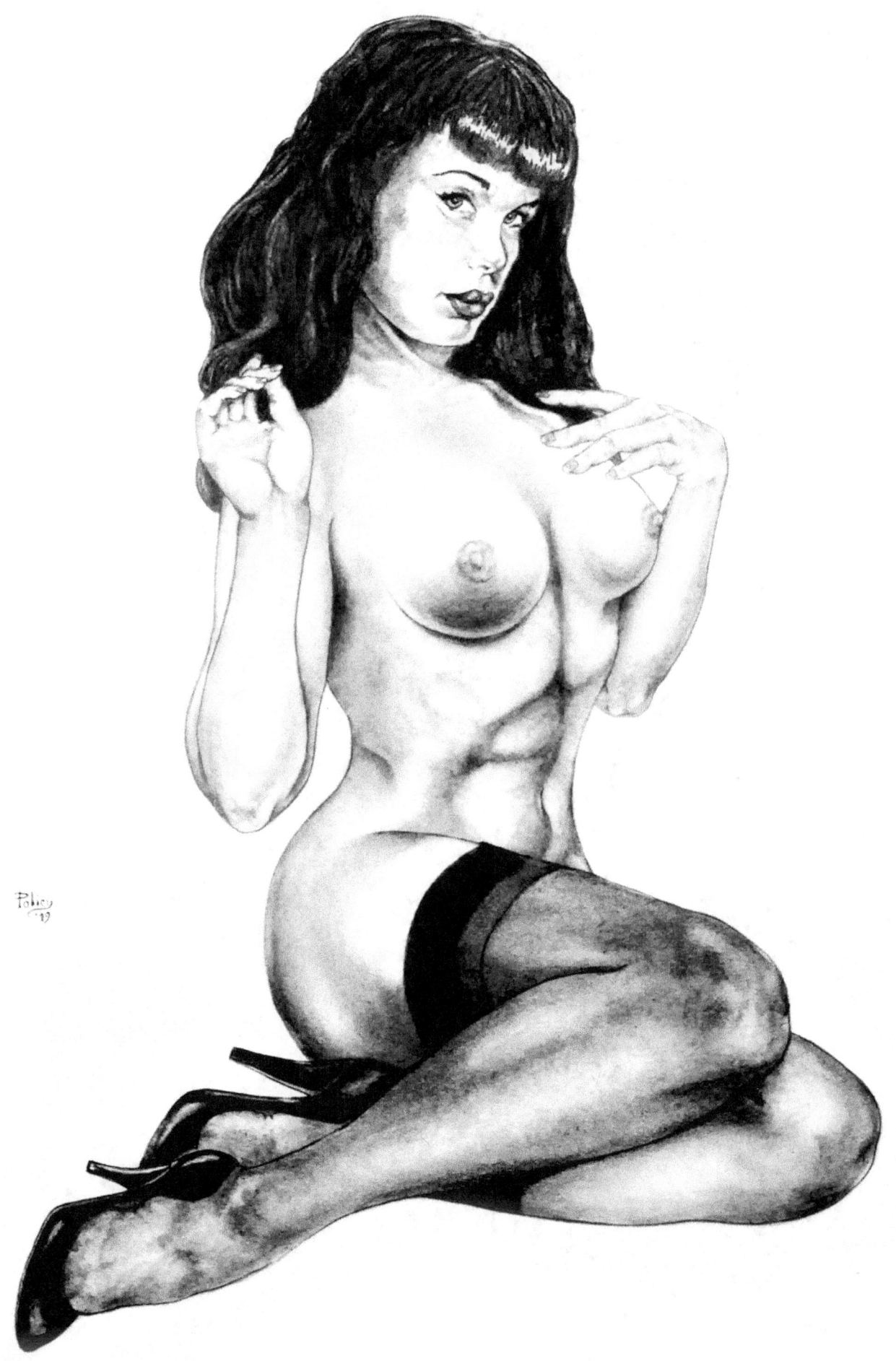

Hands Up

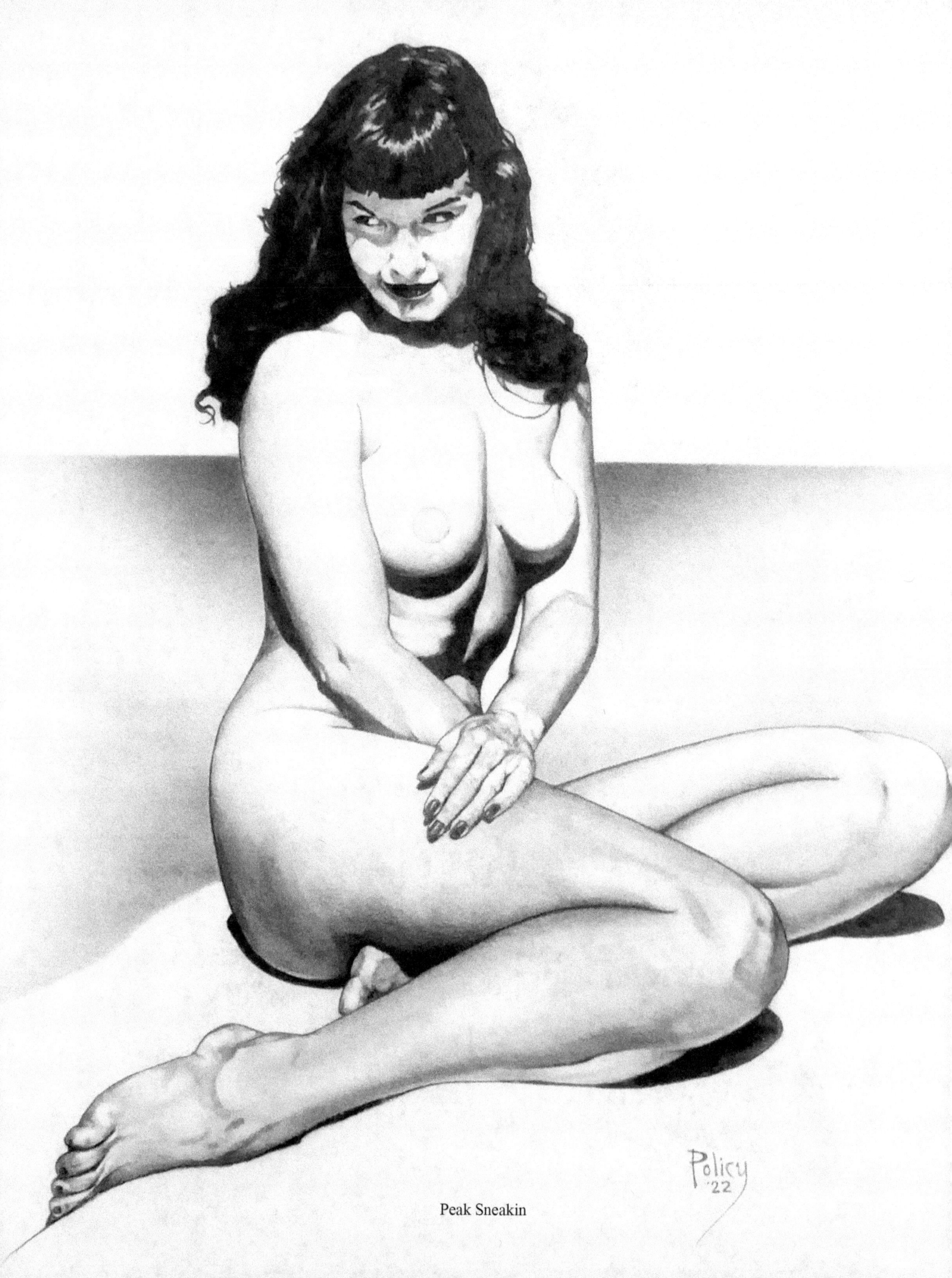
Peak Sneakin

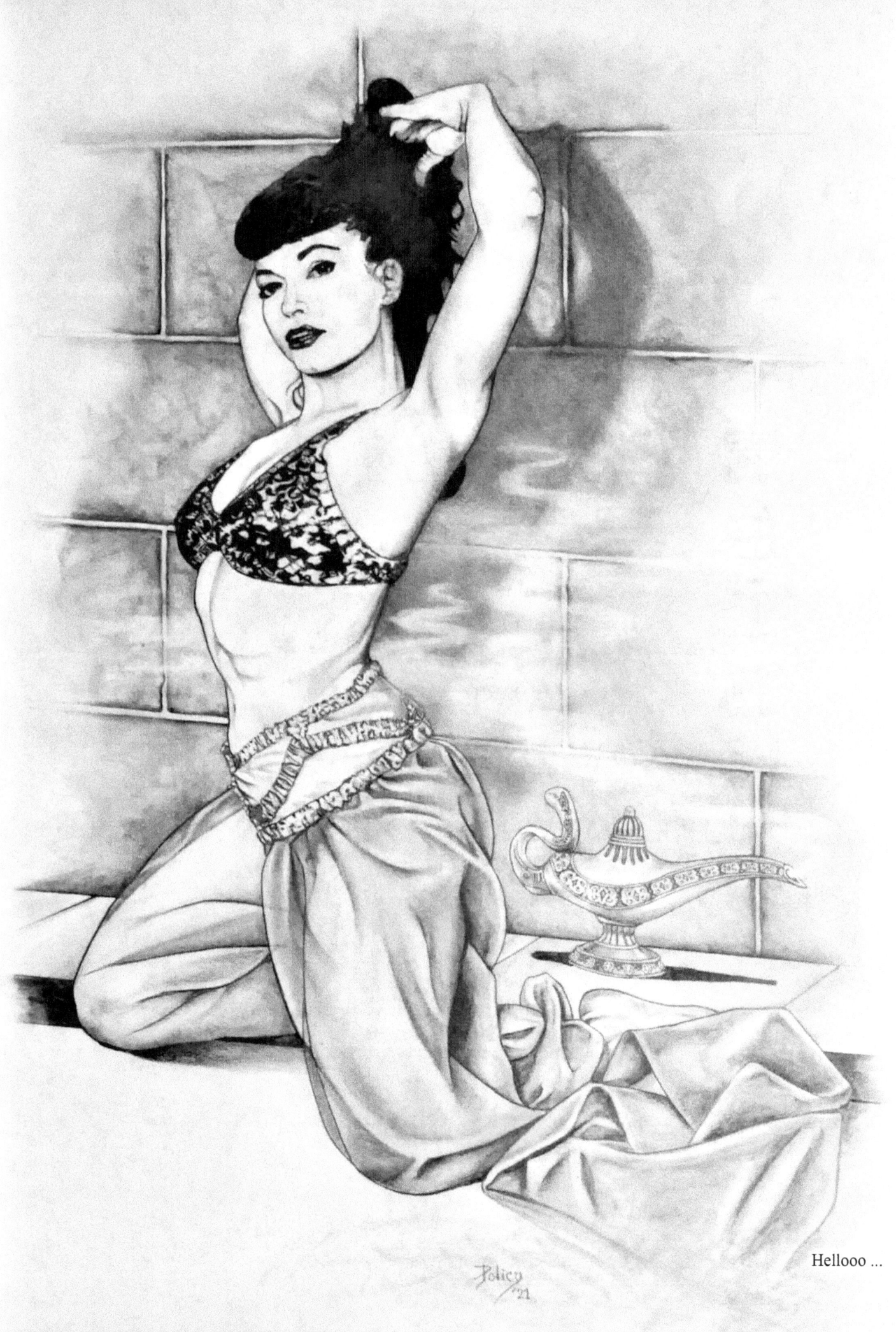

Hellooo ...

GEISHA BETTIE

Geisha Bettie

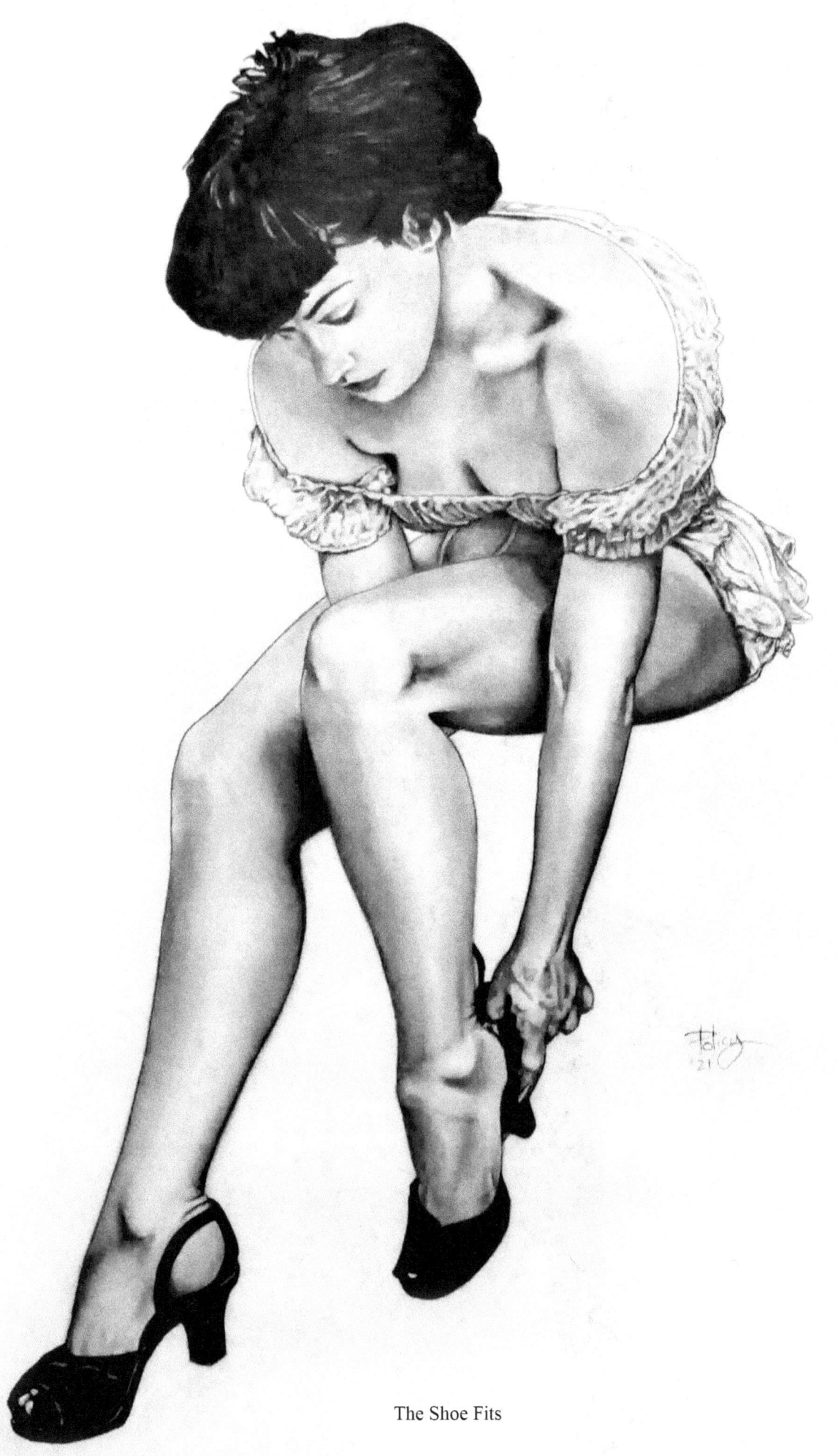

The Shoe Fits

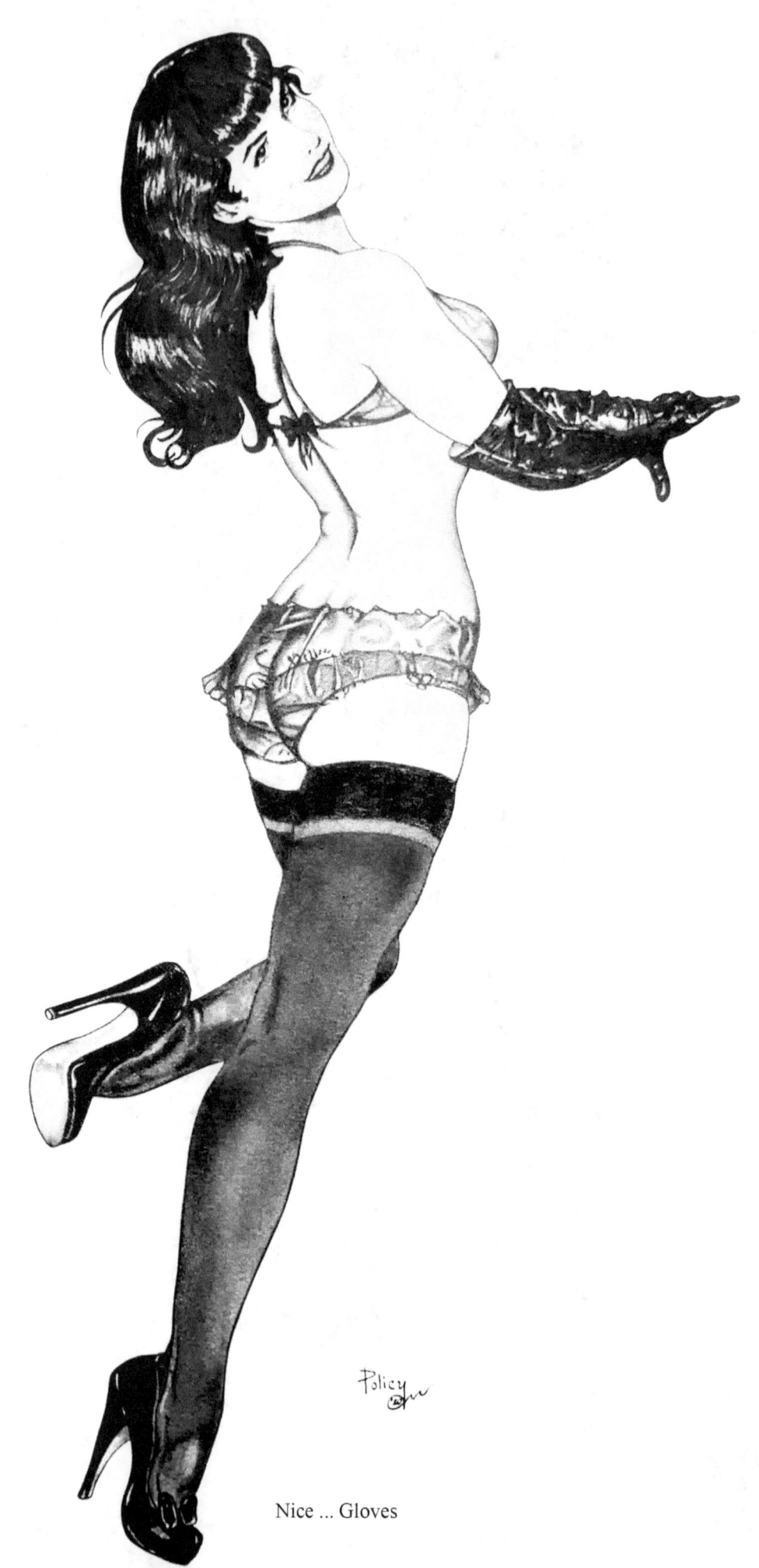

Nice ... Gloves

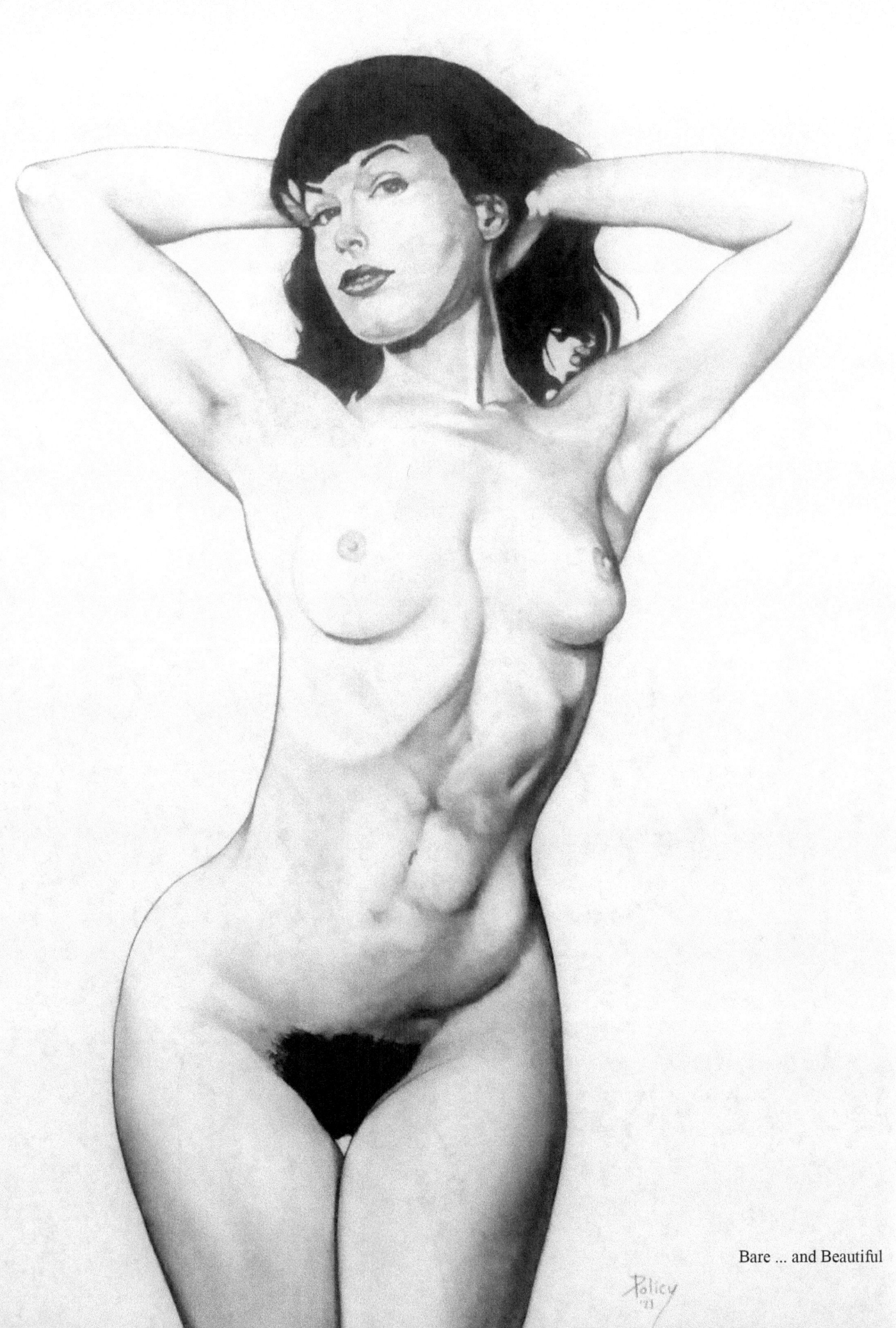

Bare ... and Beautiful

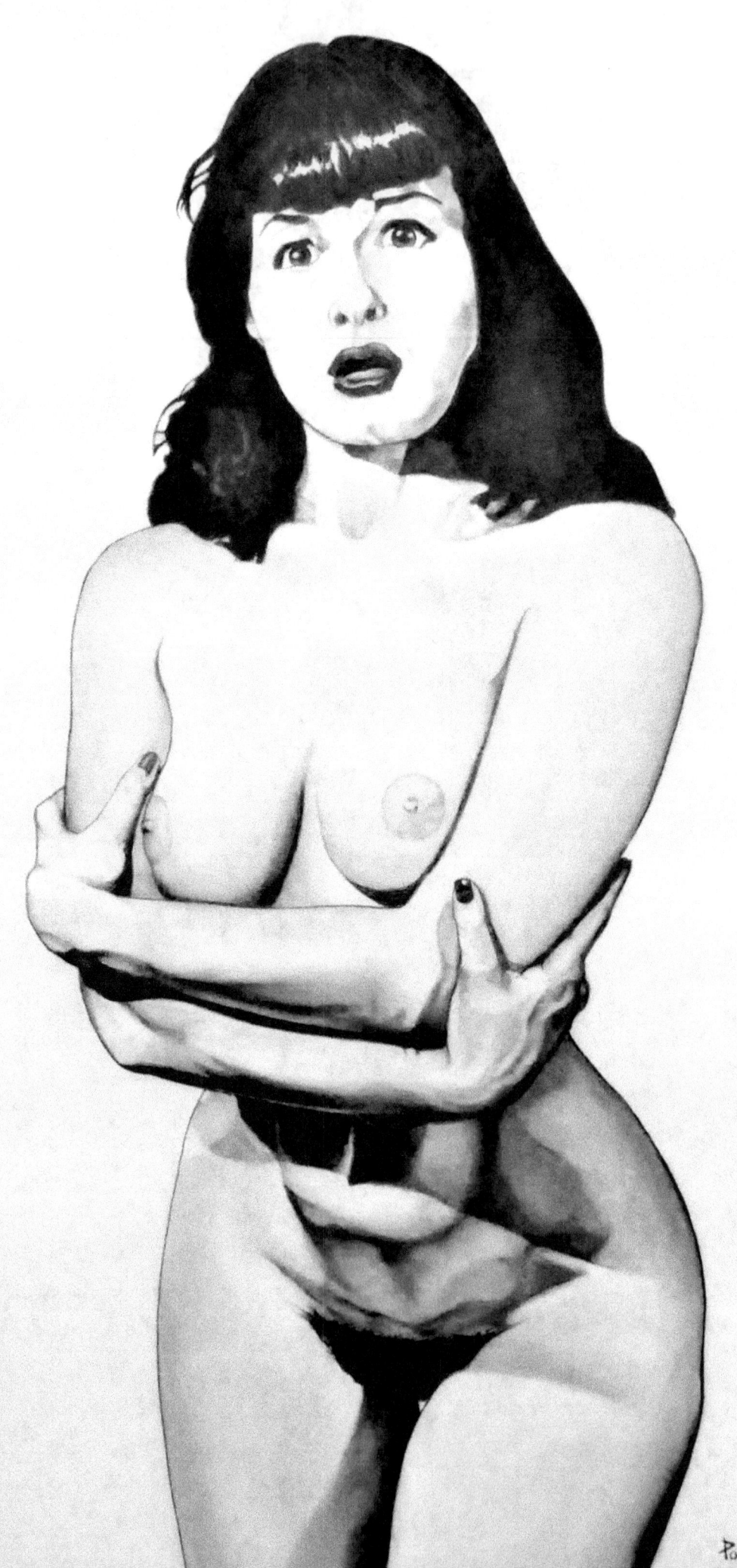

Brrr...

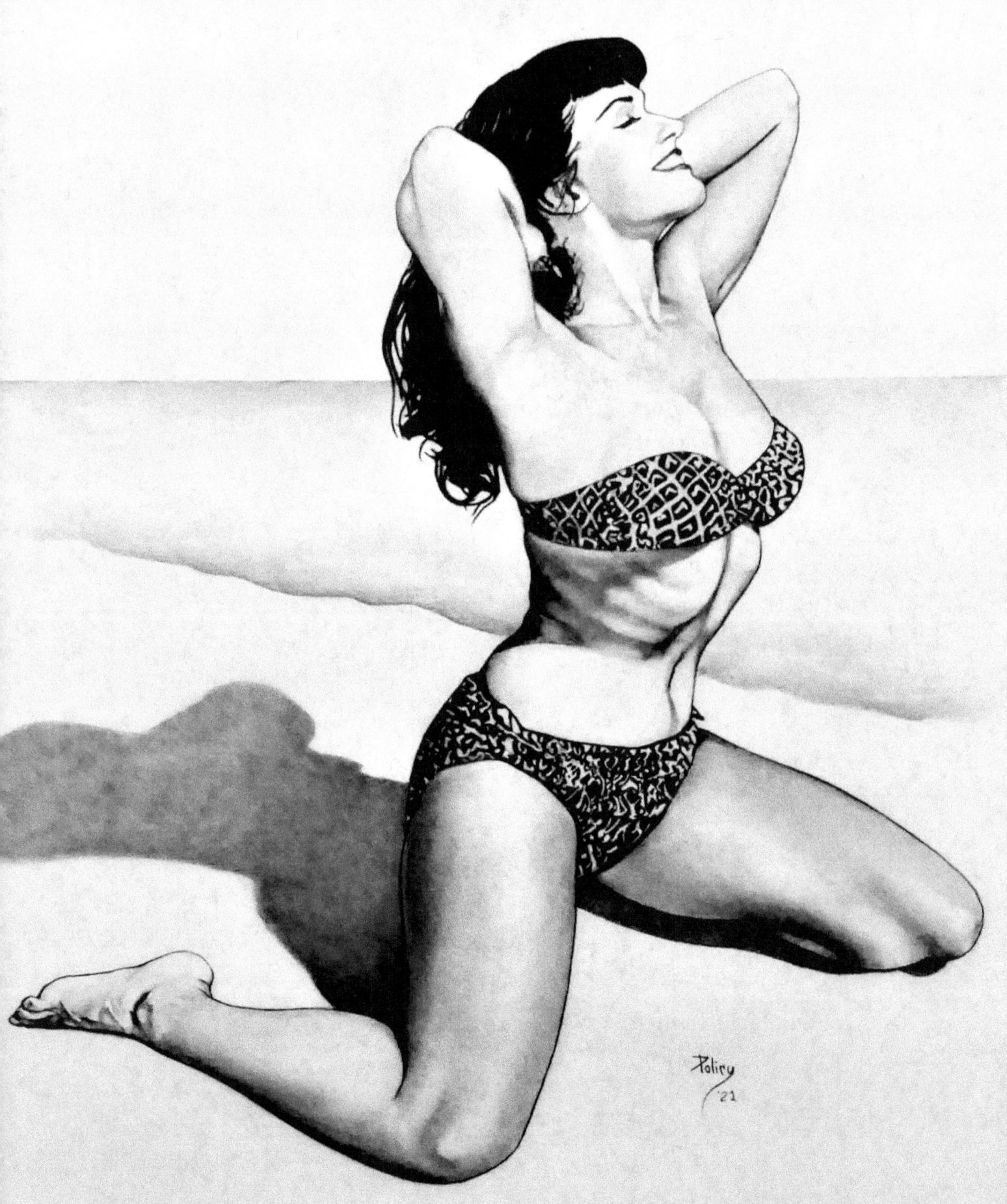

Me and My Shadow

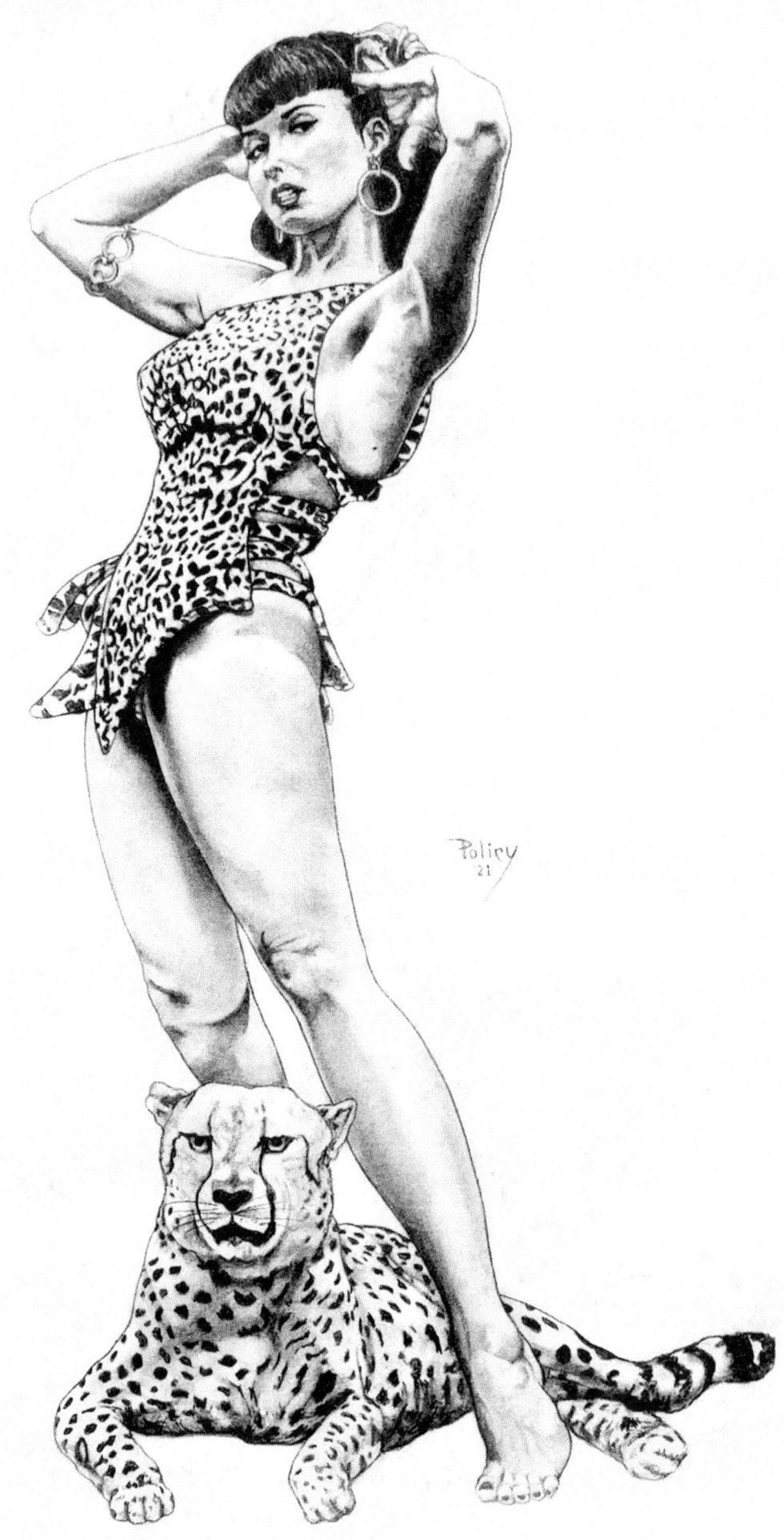

Here Kitty Kitty

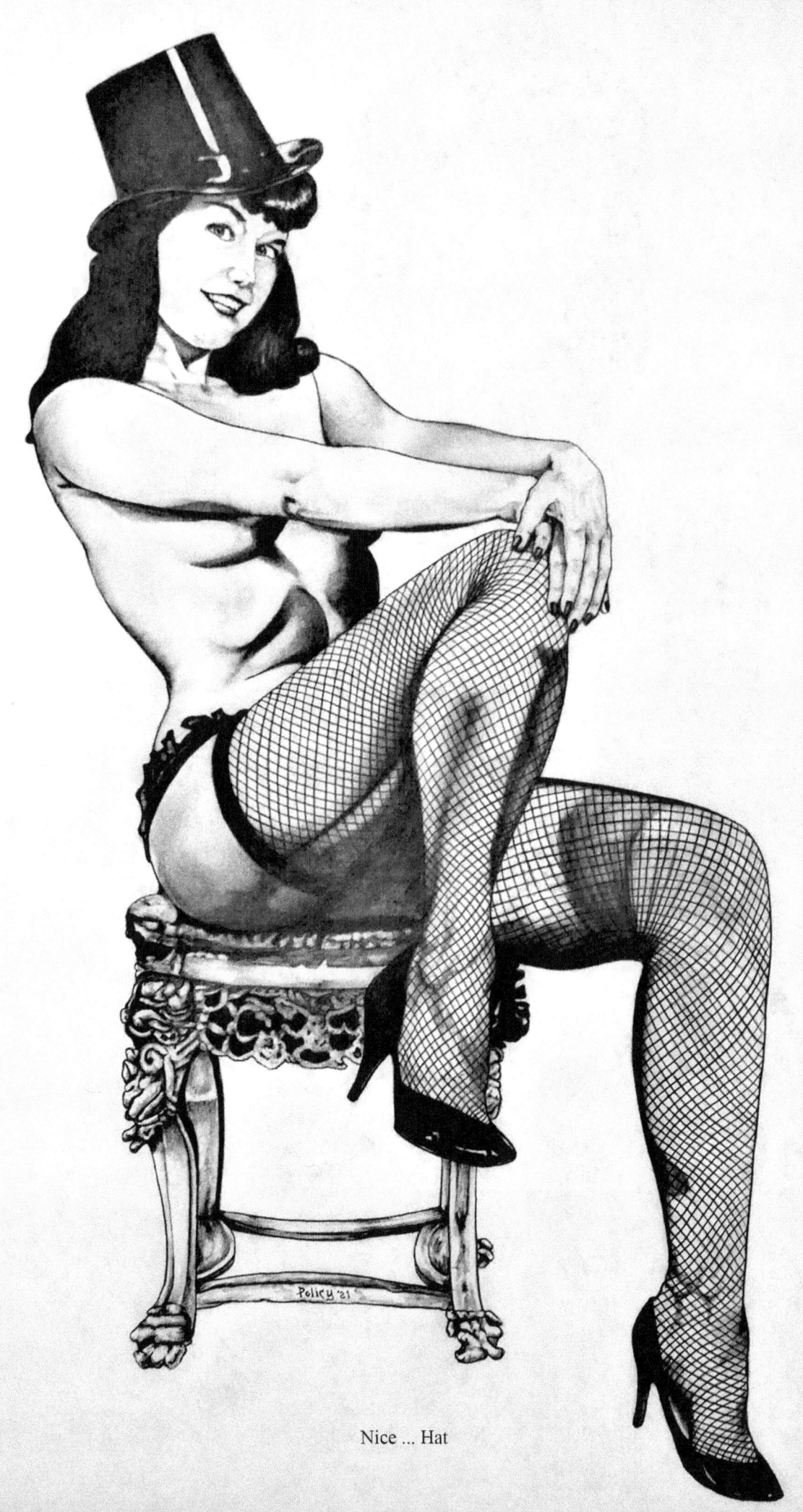

Nice ... Hat

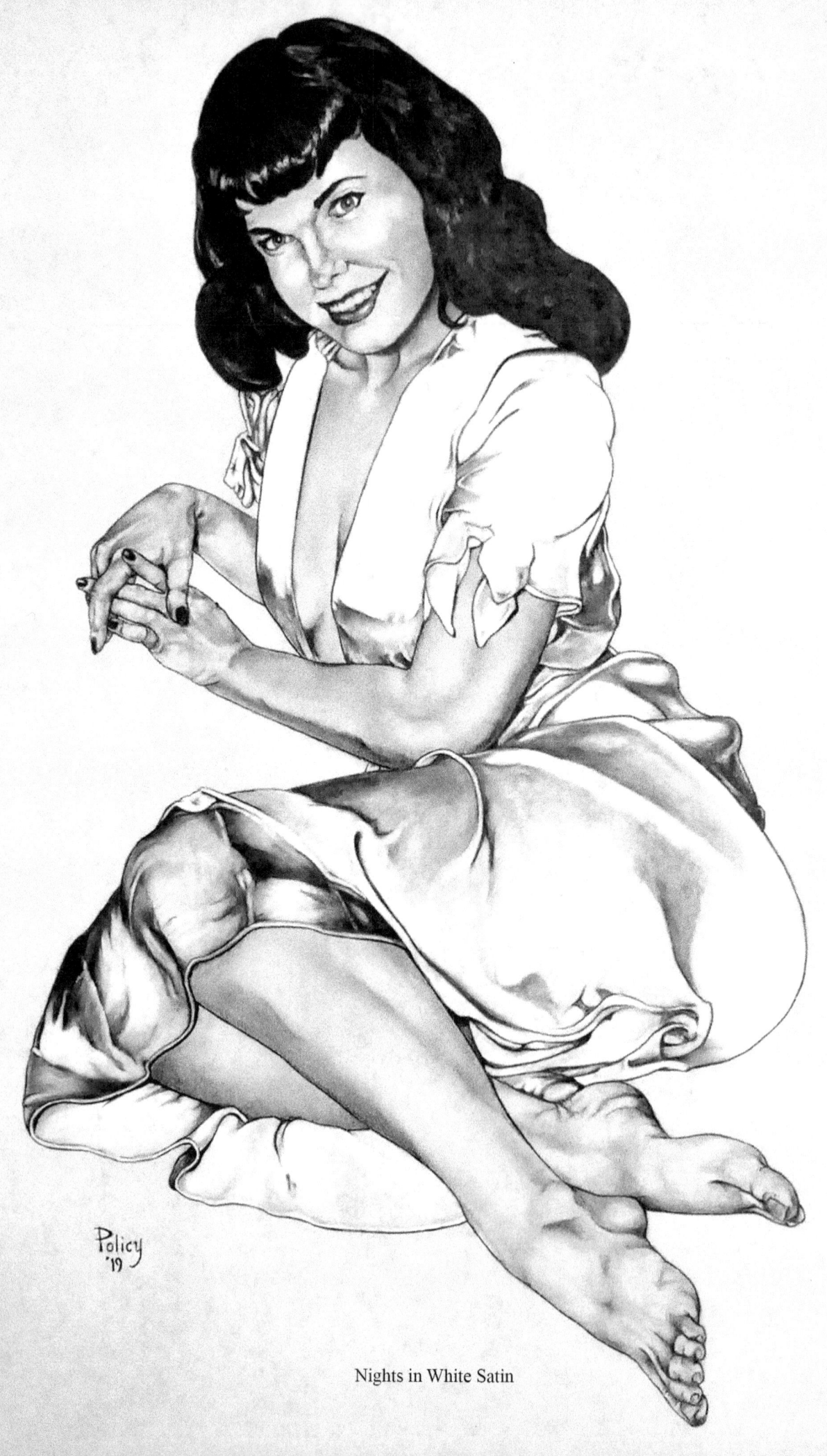

Nights in White Satin

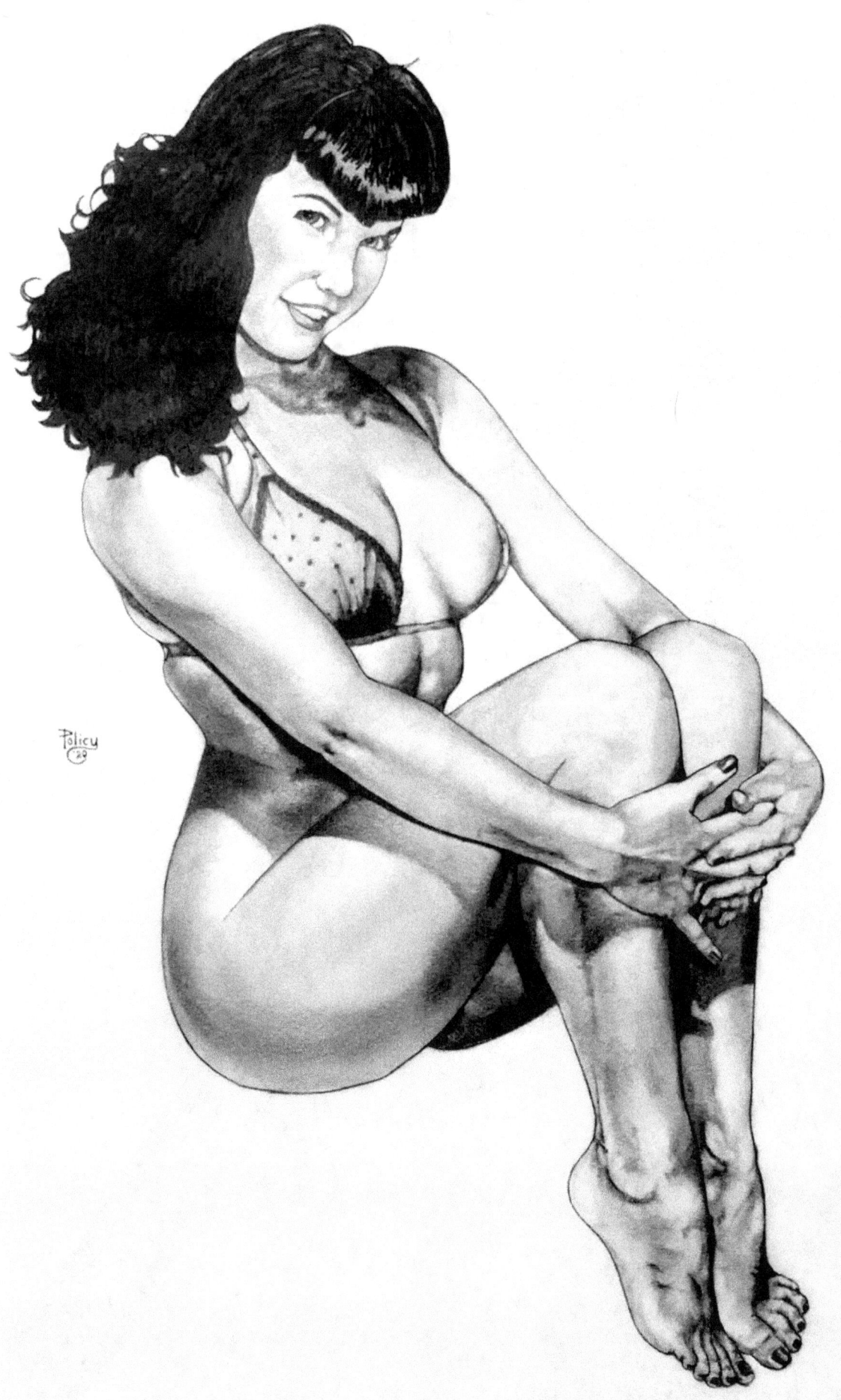

Vacation

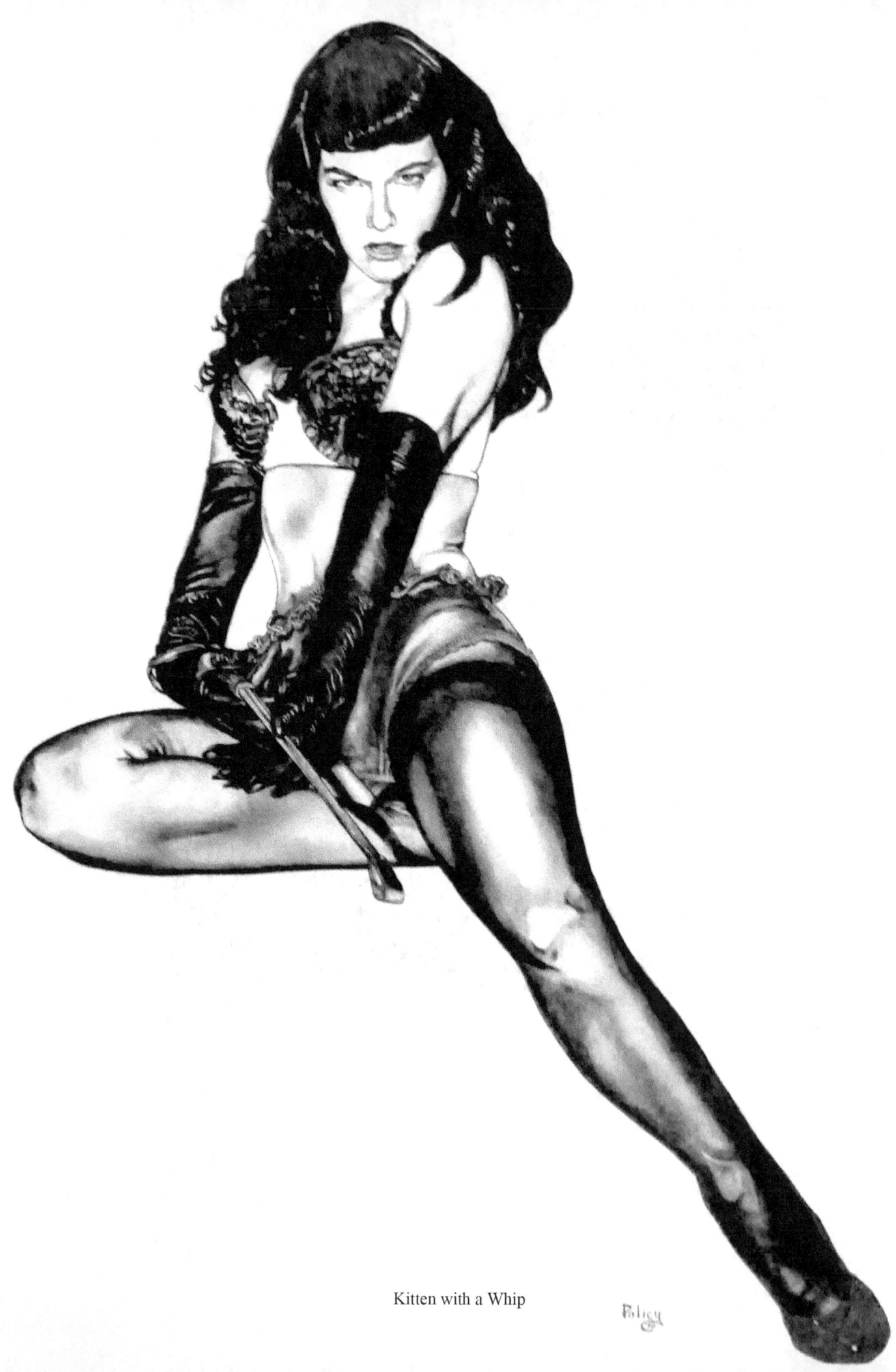

Kitten with a Whip

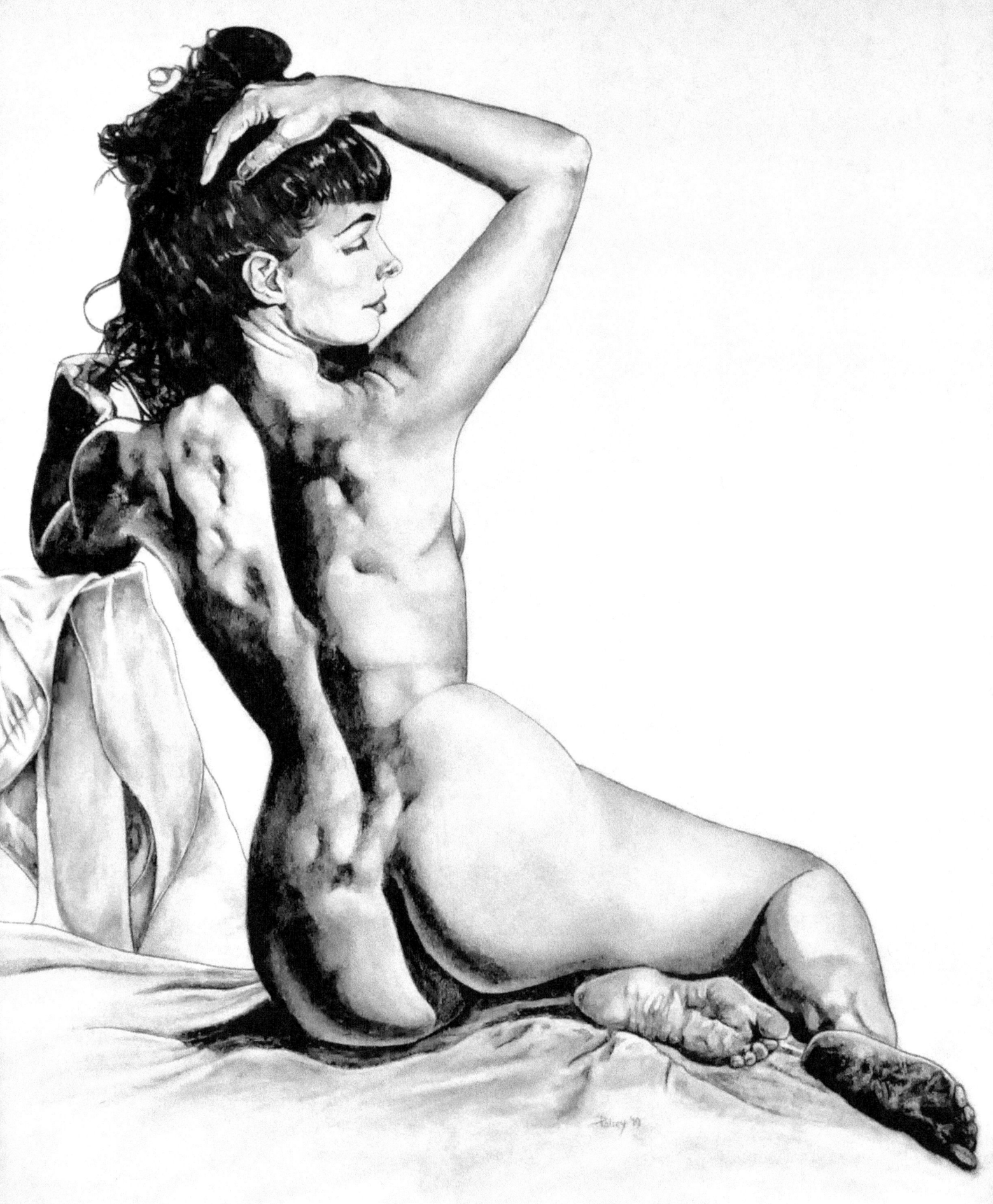

Right Back Atcha

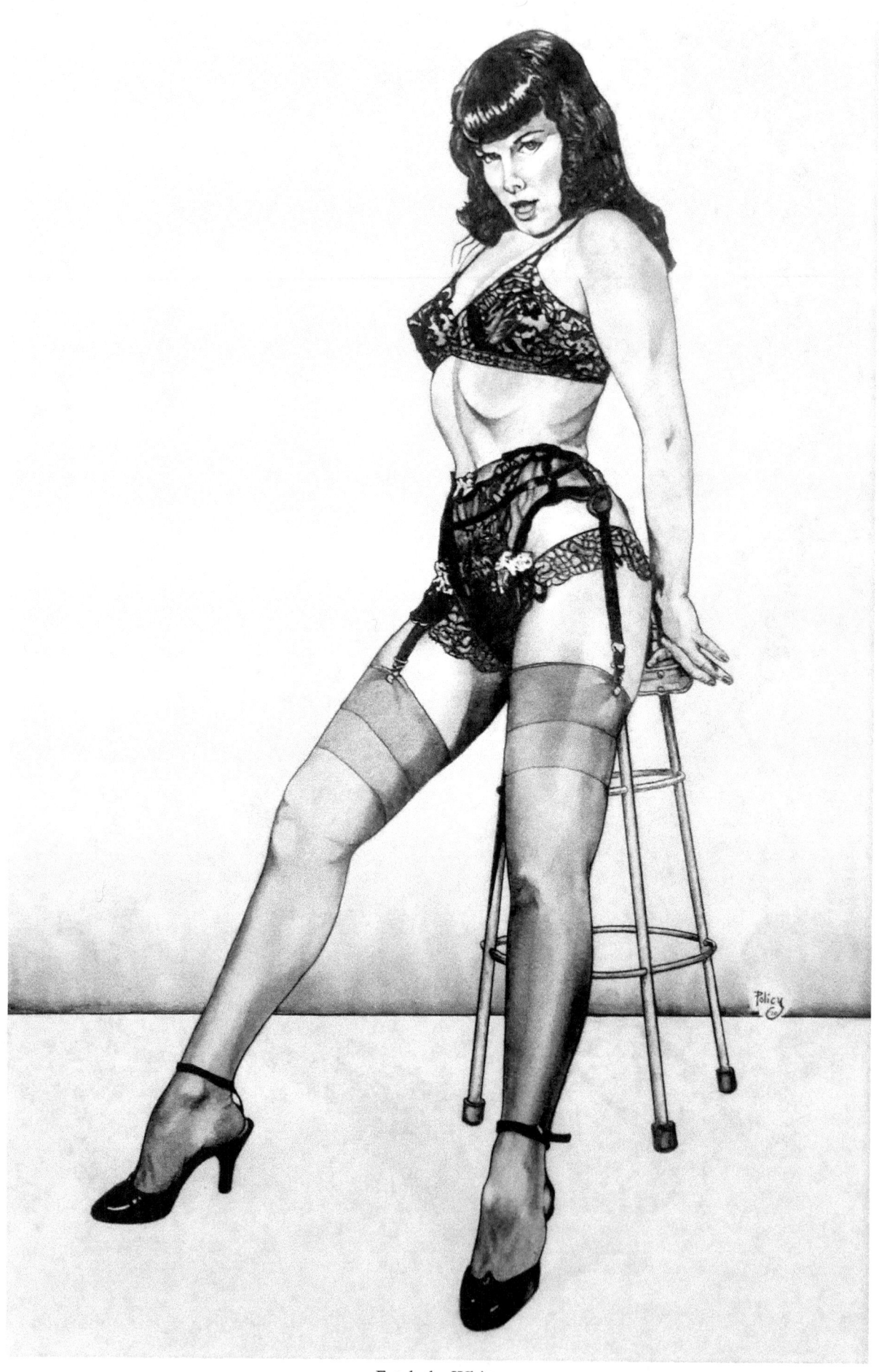

Fetch the Whip

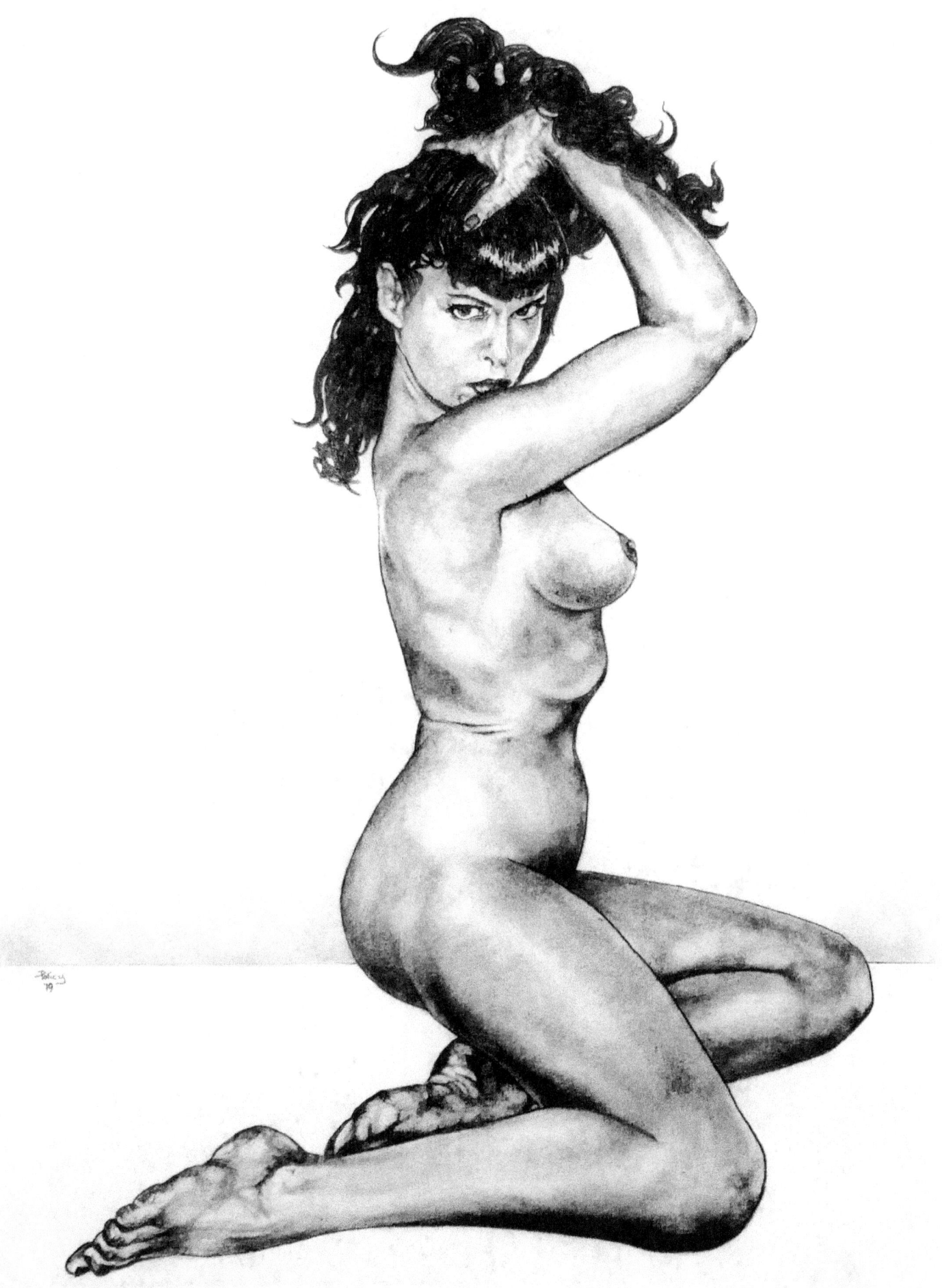

That Look

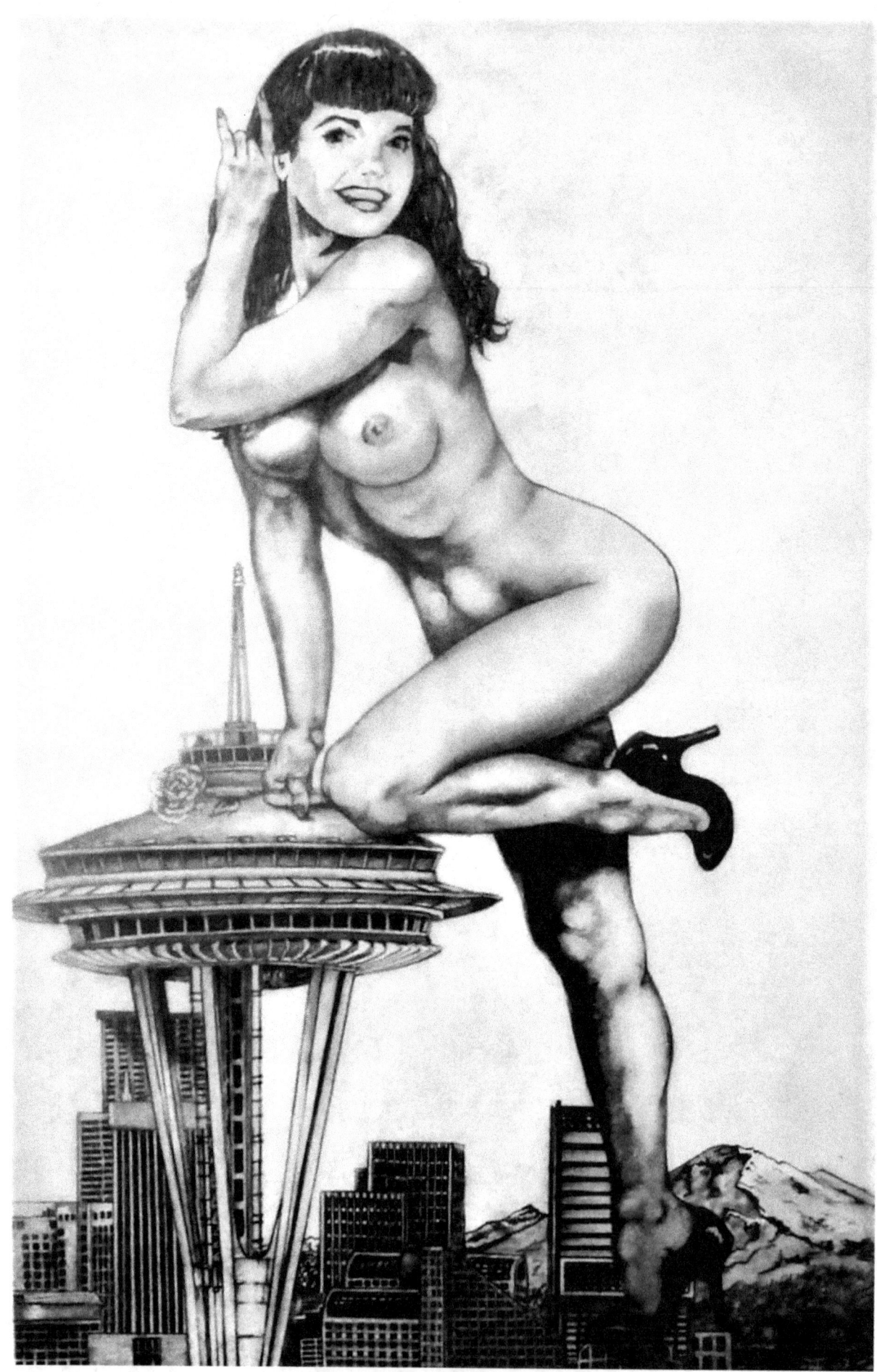

Scenic Mt. Rainier

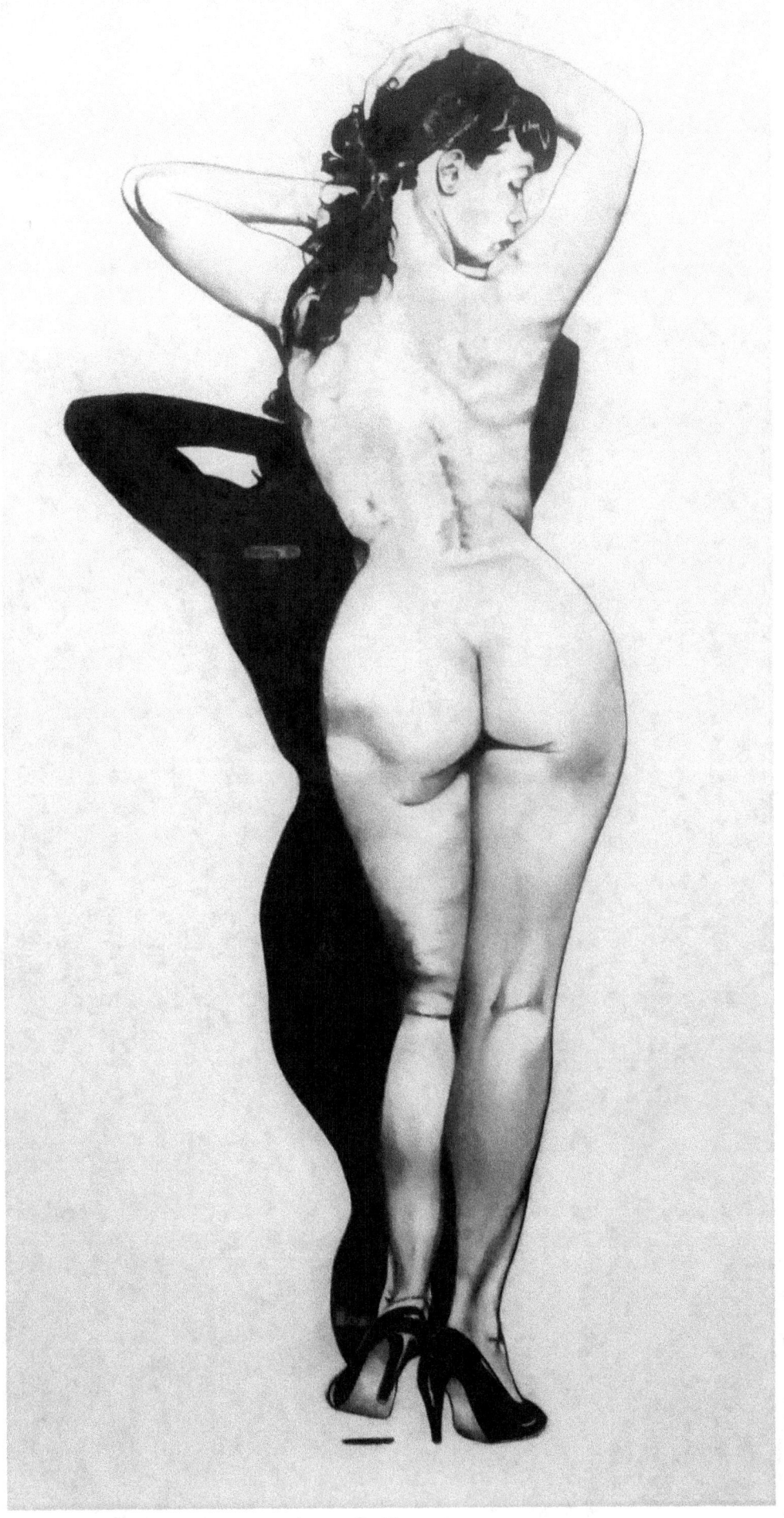

Go Figure

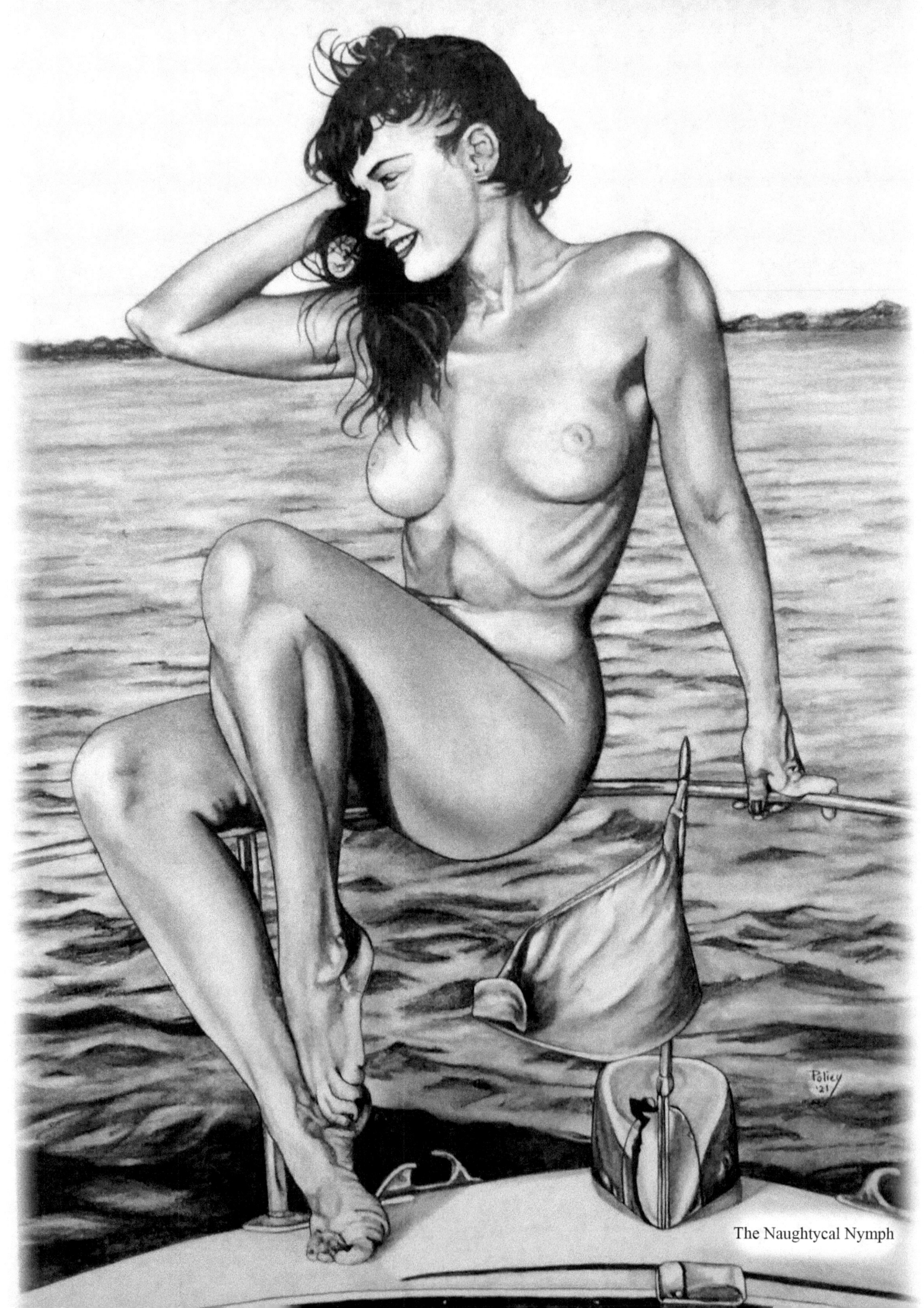

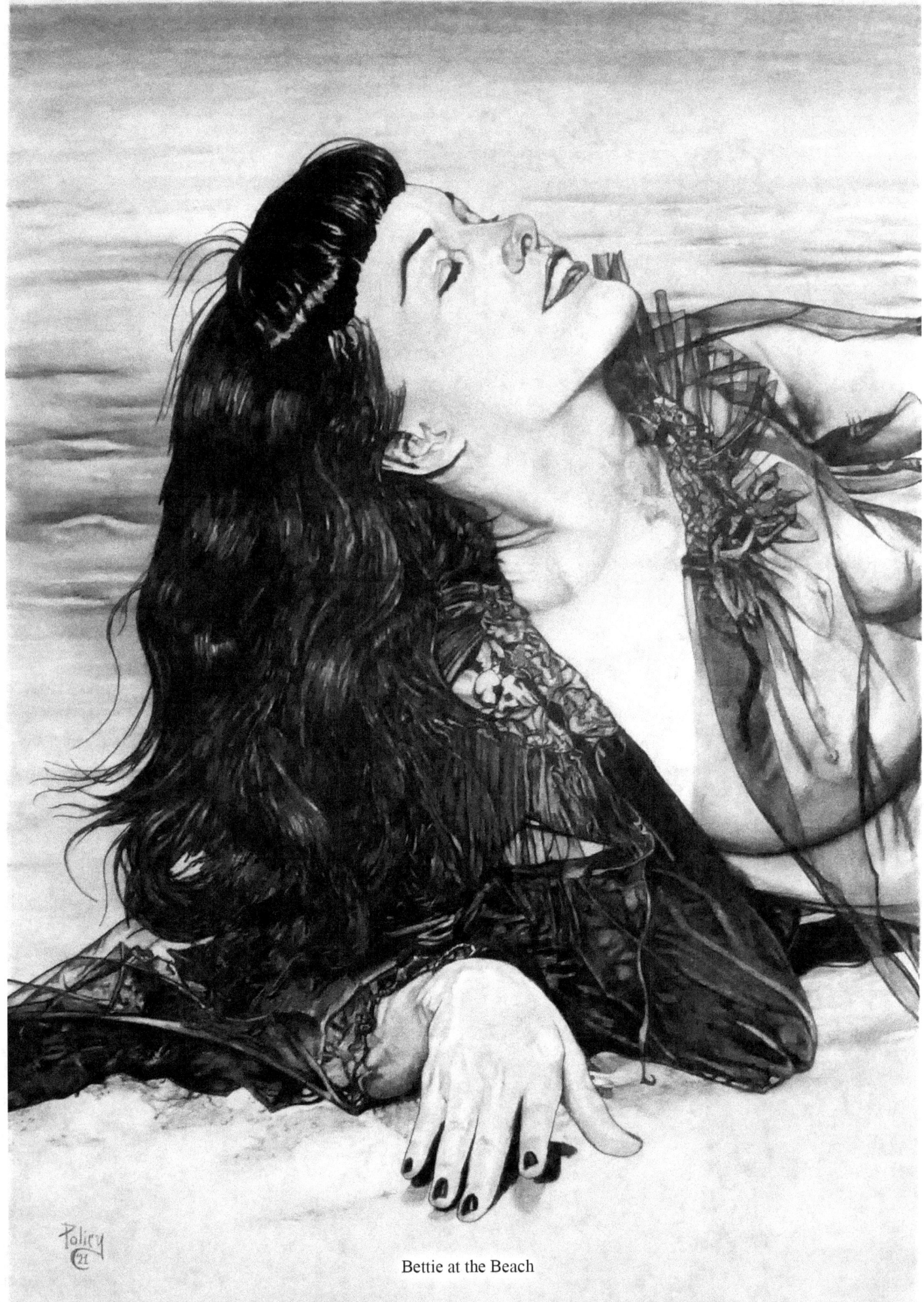

Bettie at the Beach

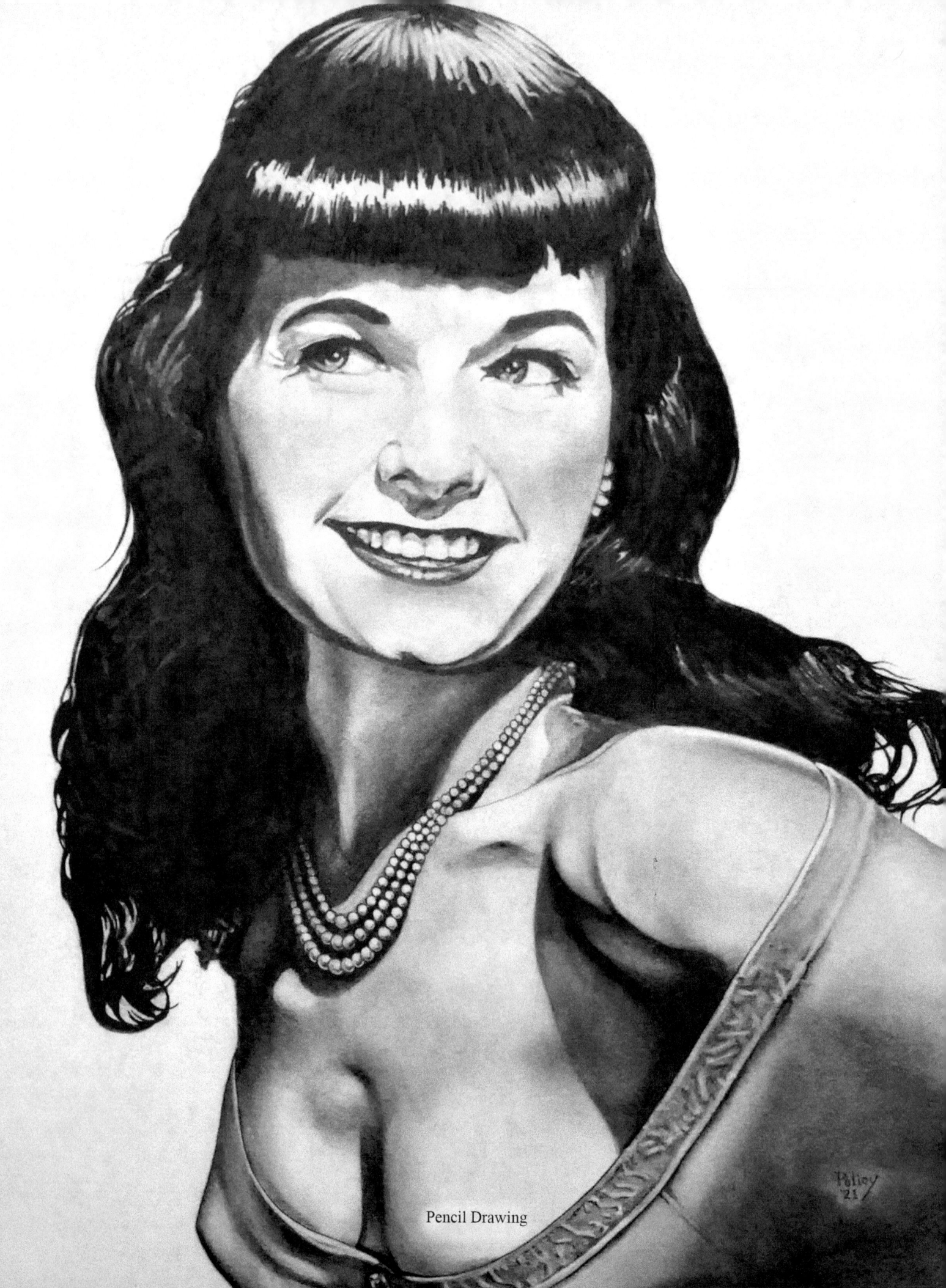
Pencil Drawing

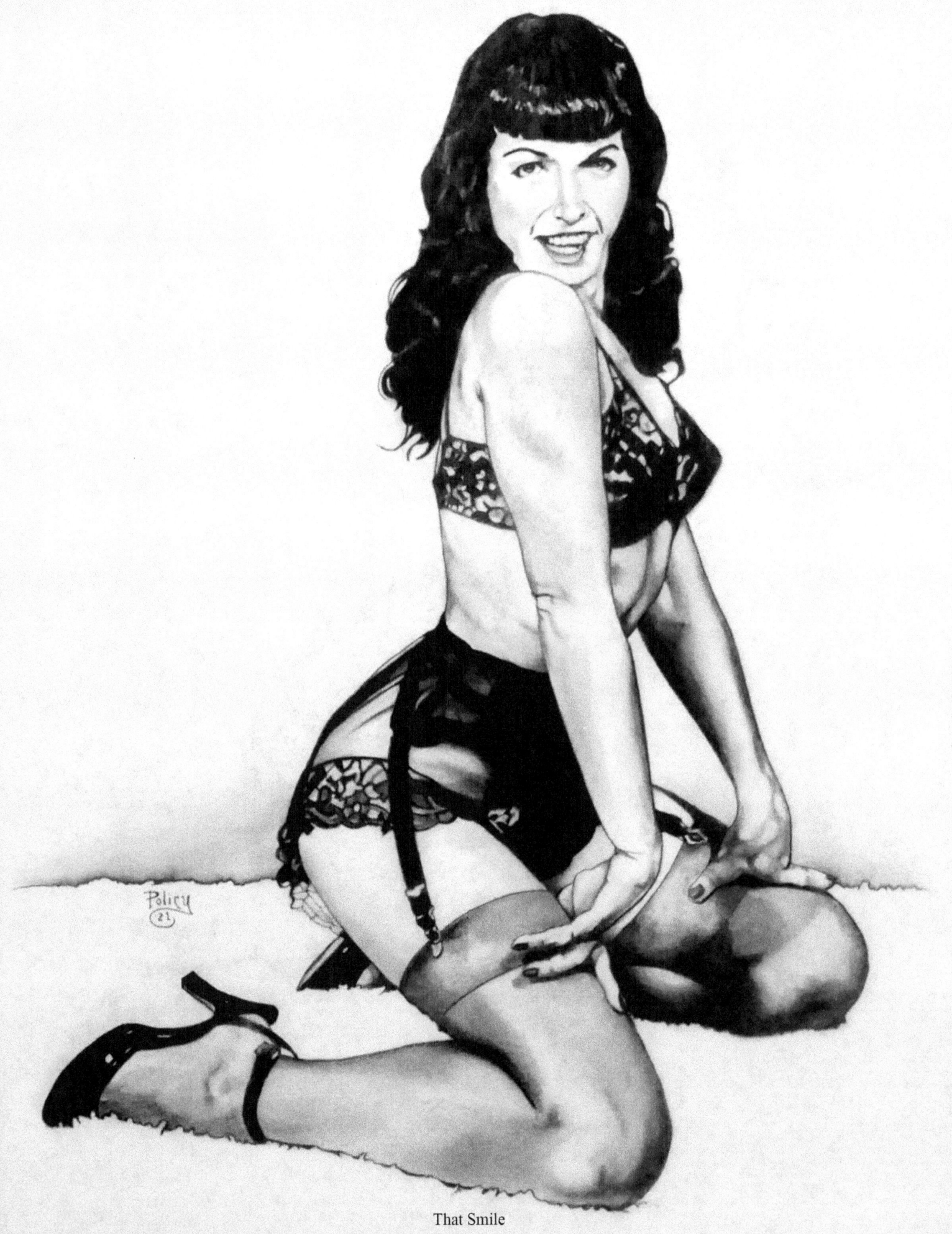

That Smile

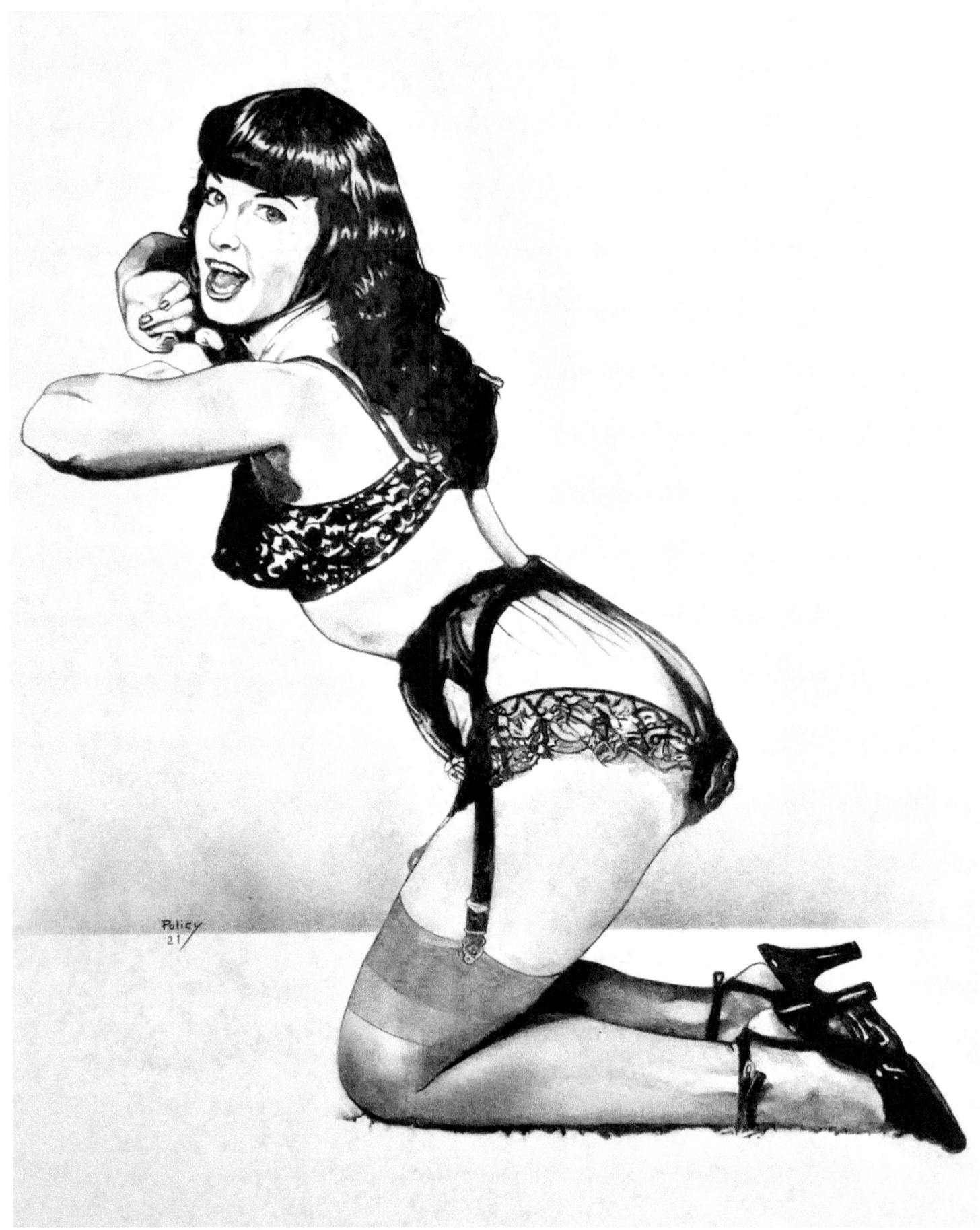

Just Showing Off II

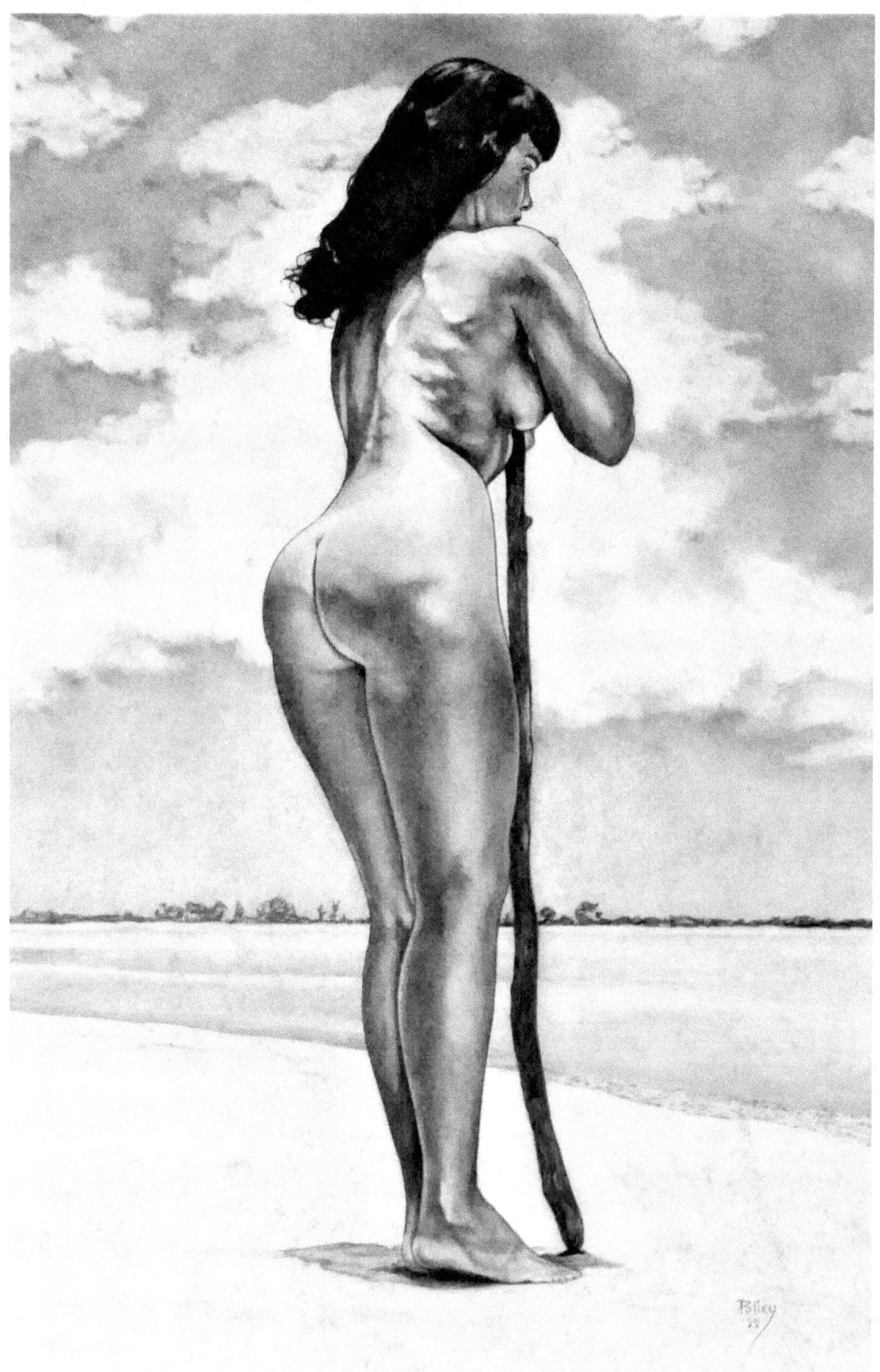

Lady of the Lake

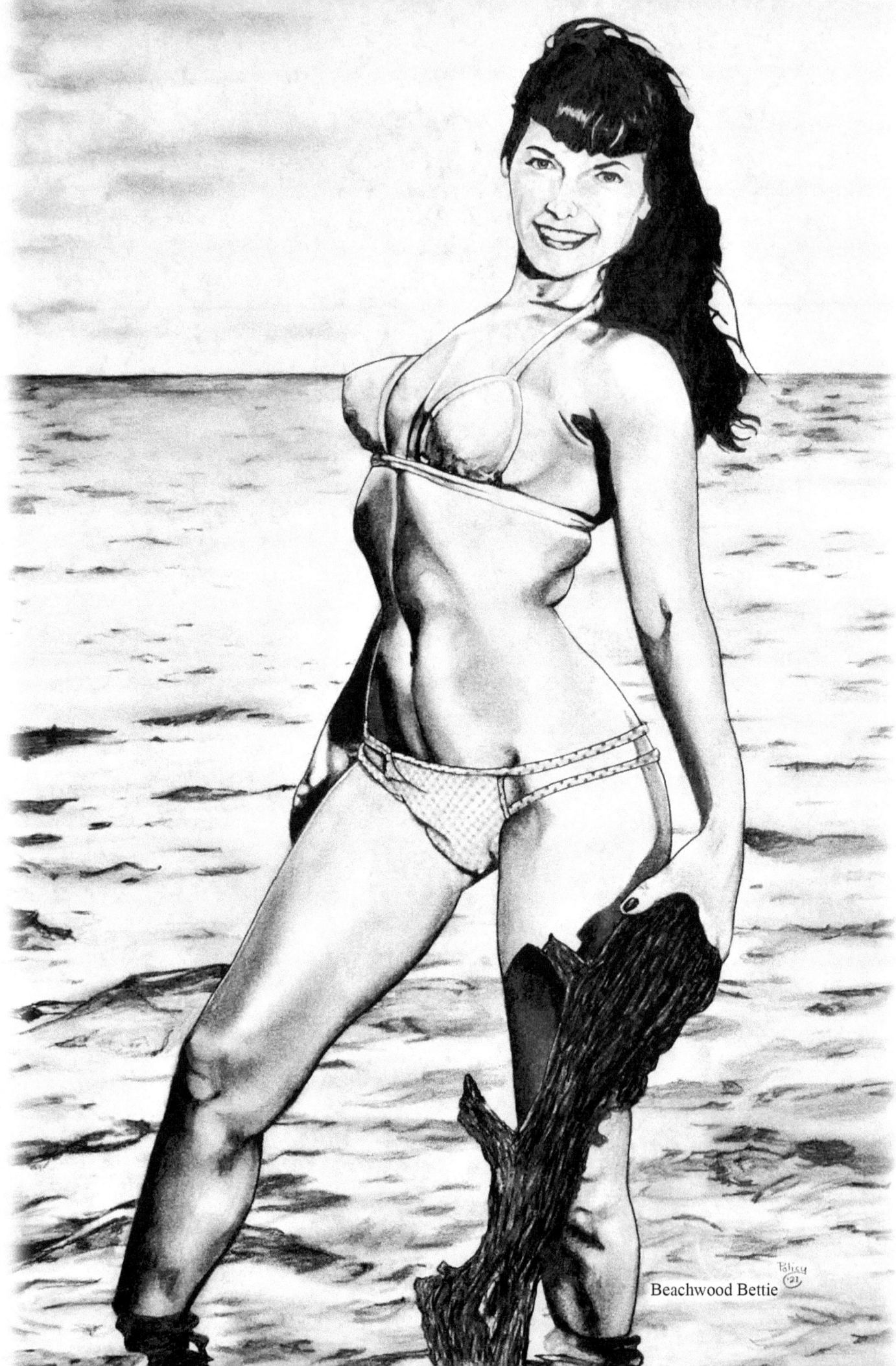

Beachwood Bettie

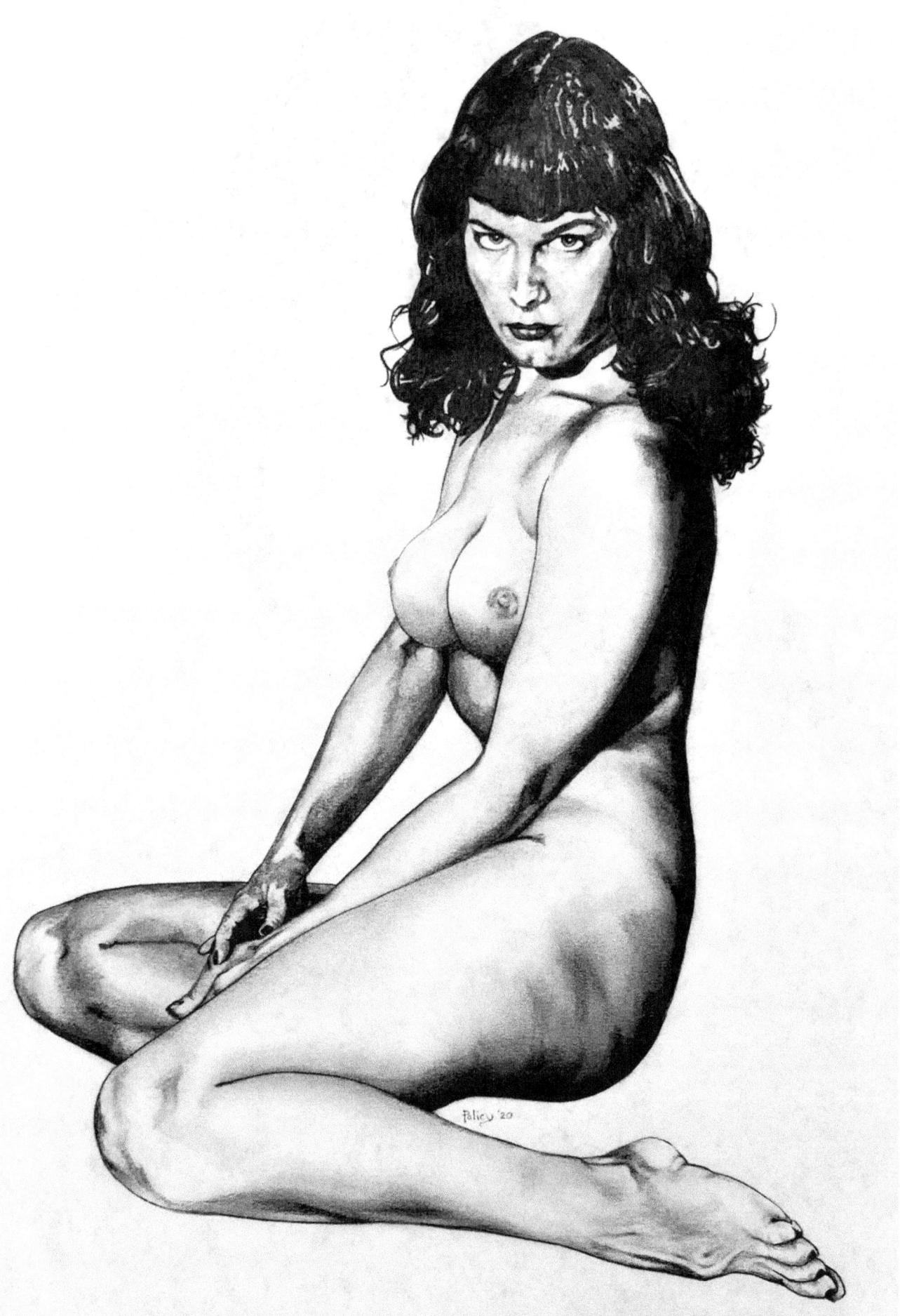
But Seriously, Folks

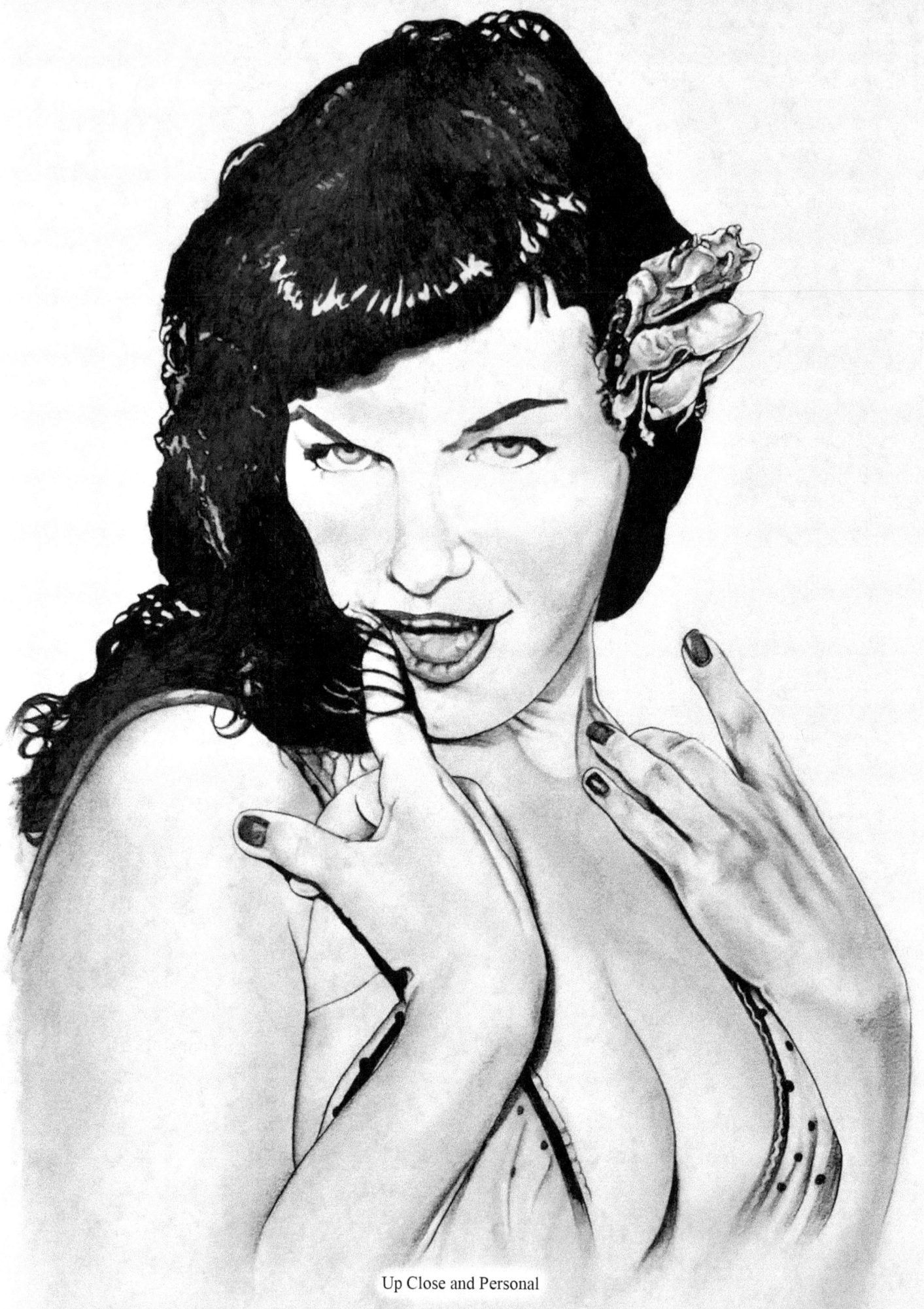
Up Close and Personal

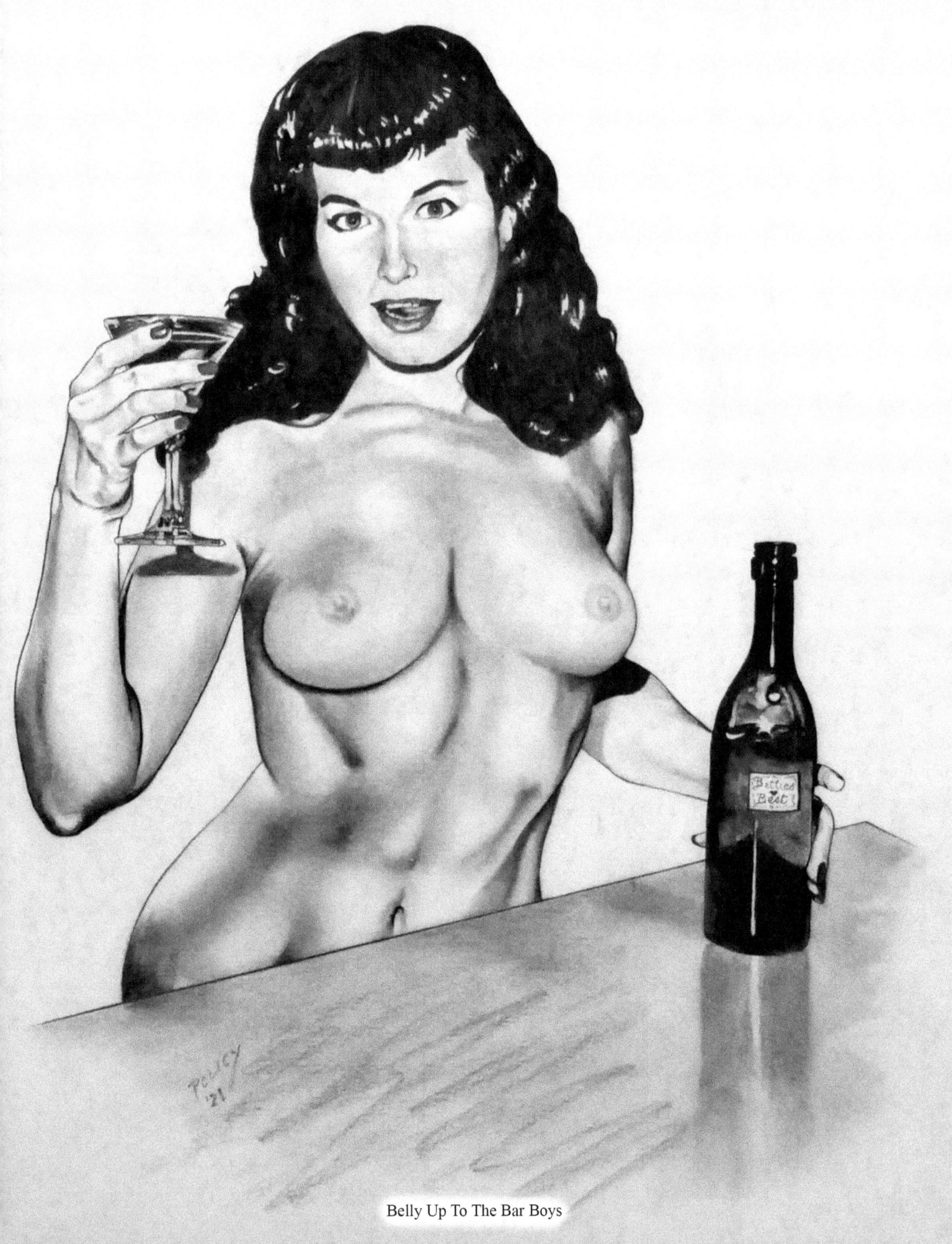
Belly Up To The Bar Boys

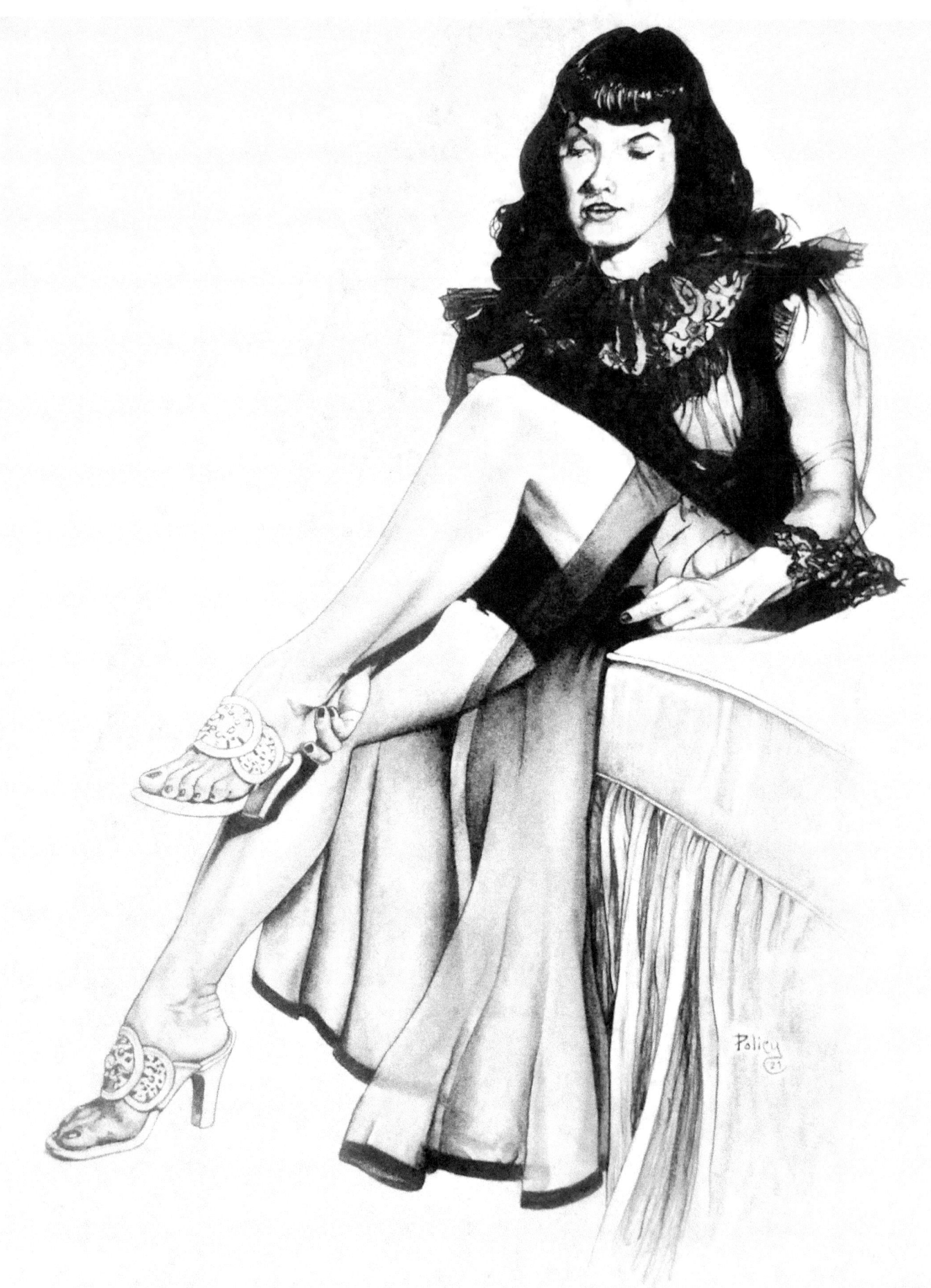

Perfect Fit

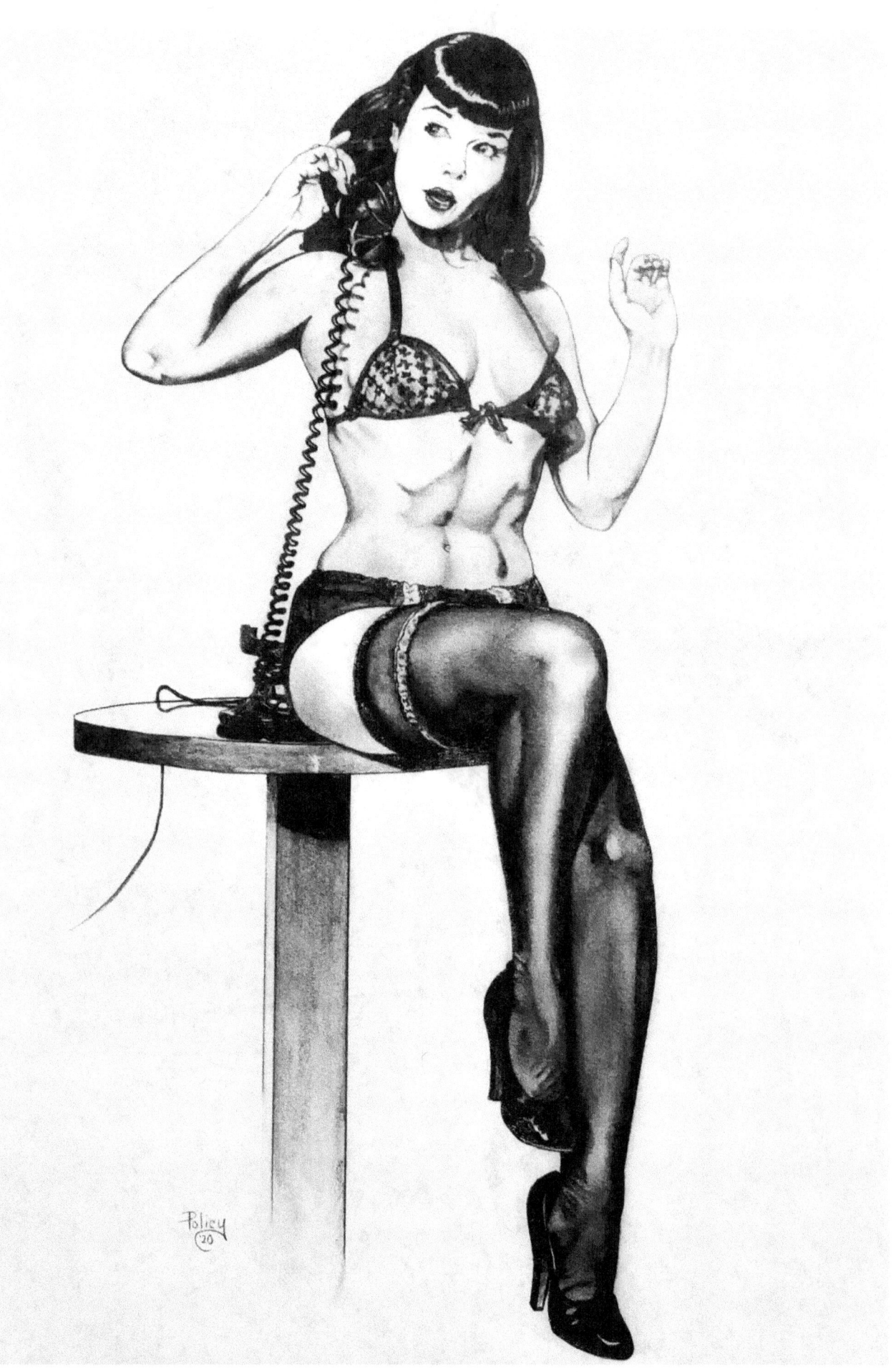

It's Called A Landline, Kids

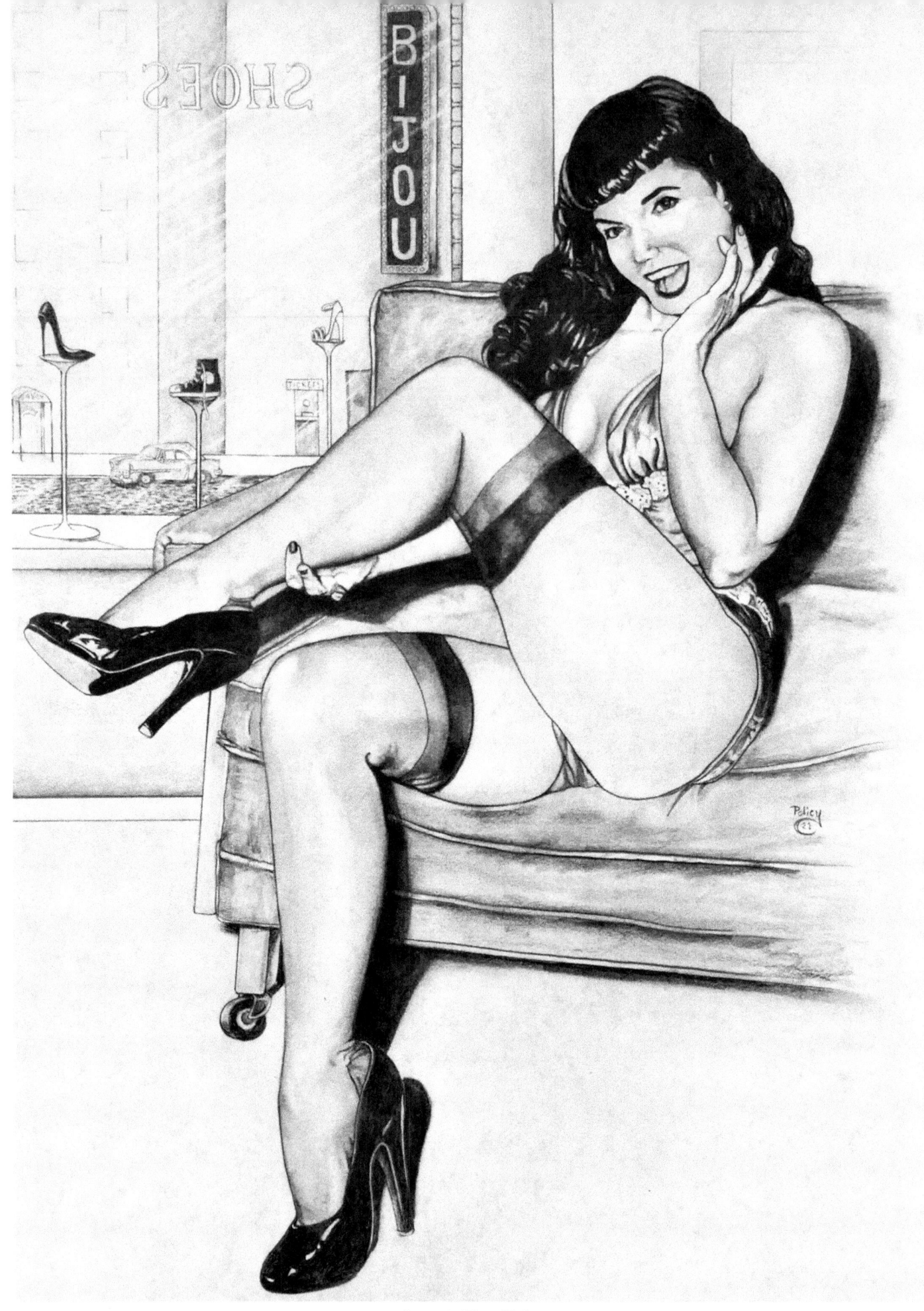

Love At First Sight

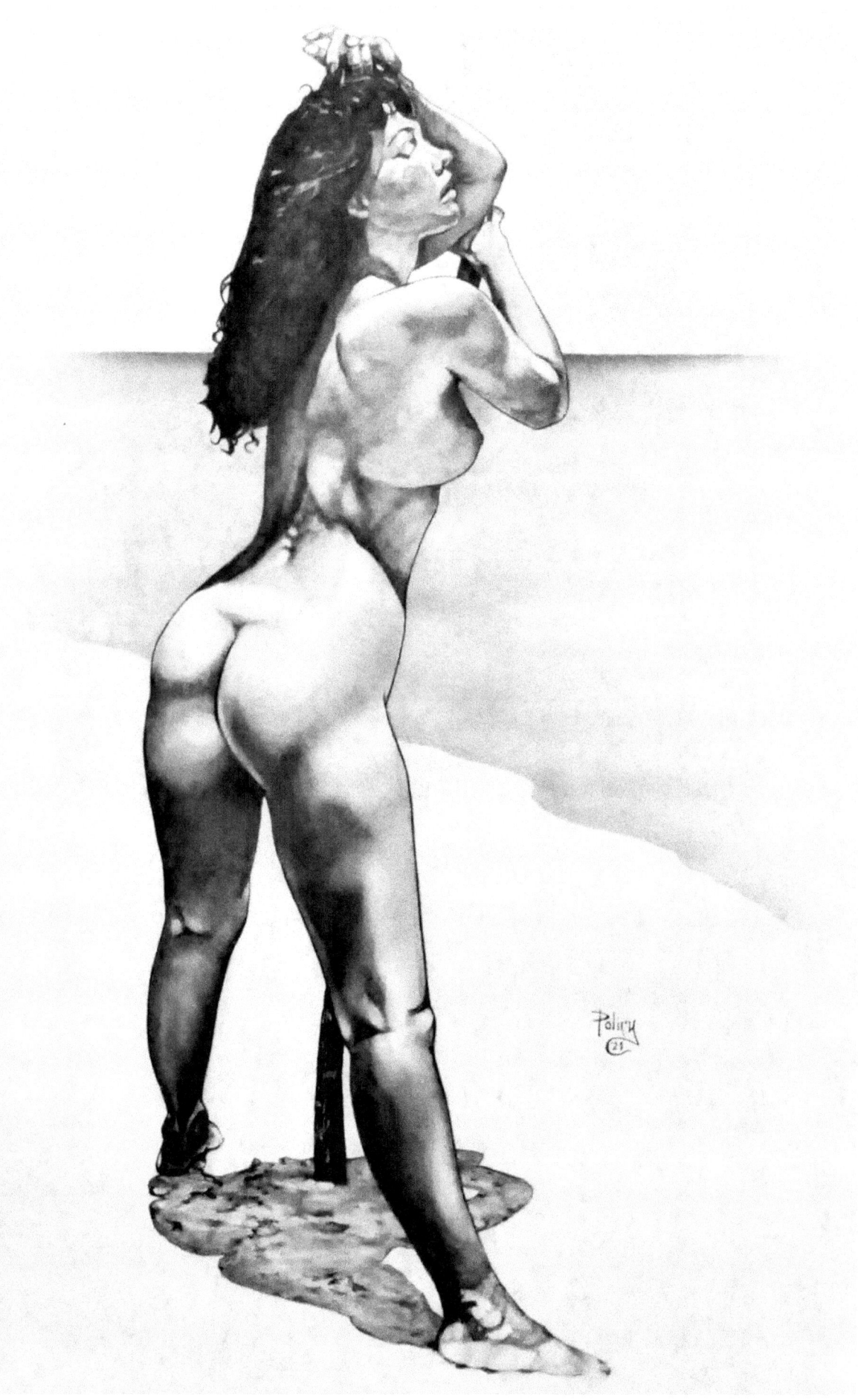
Beach Bum

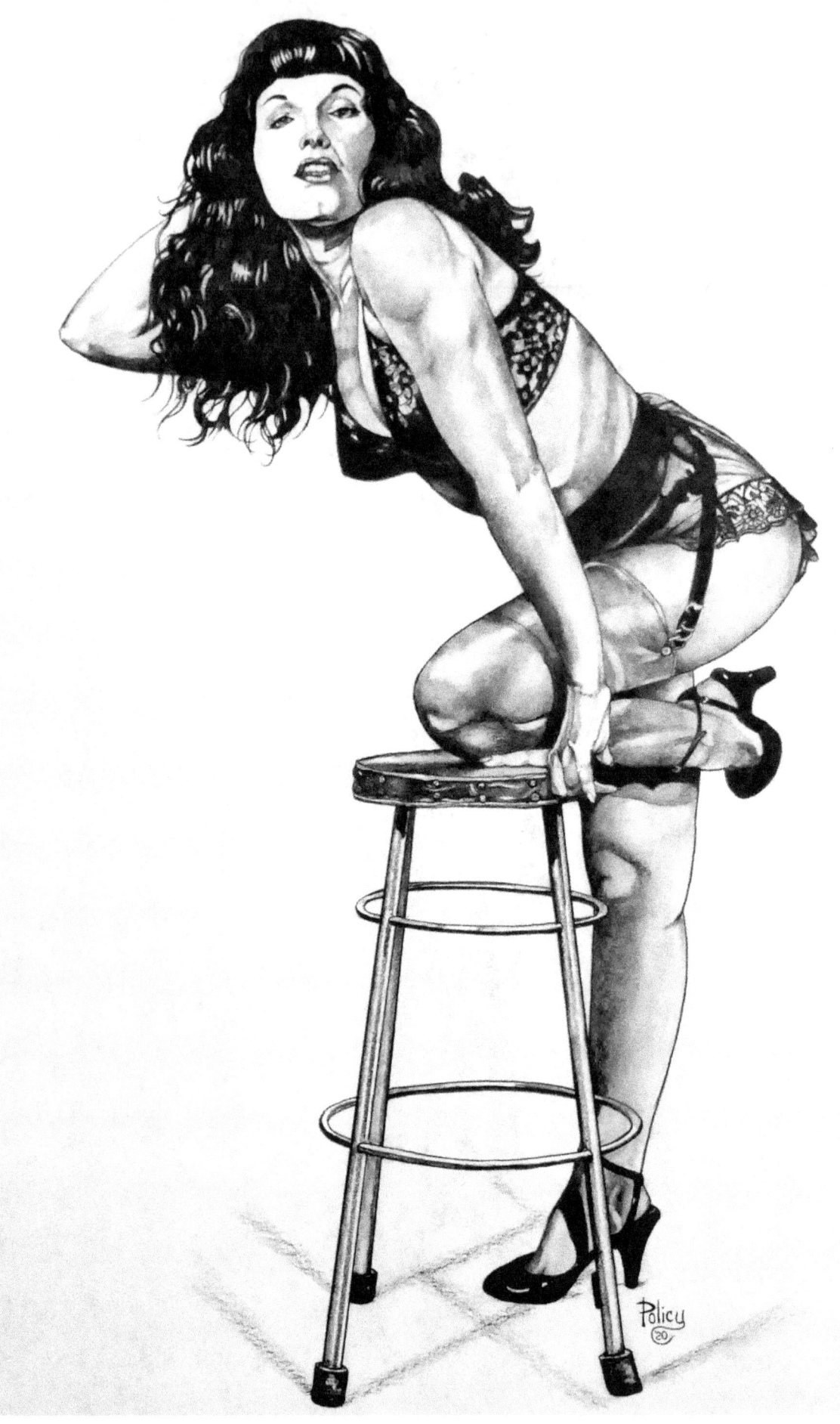
Home of the Better Barstool

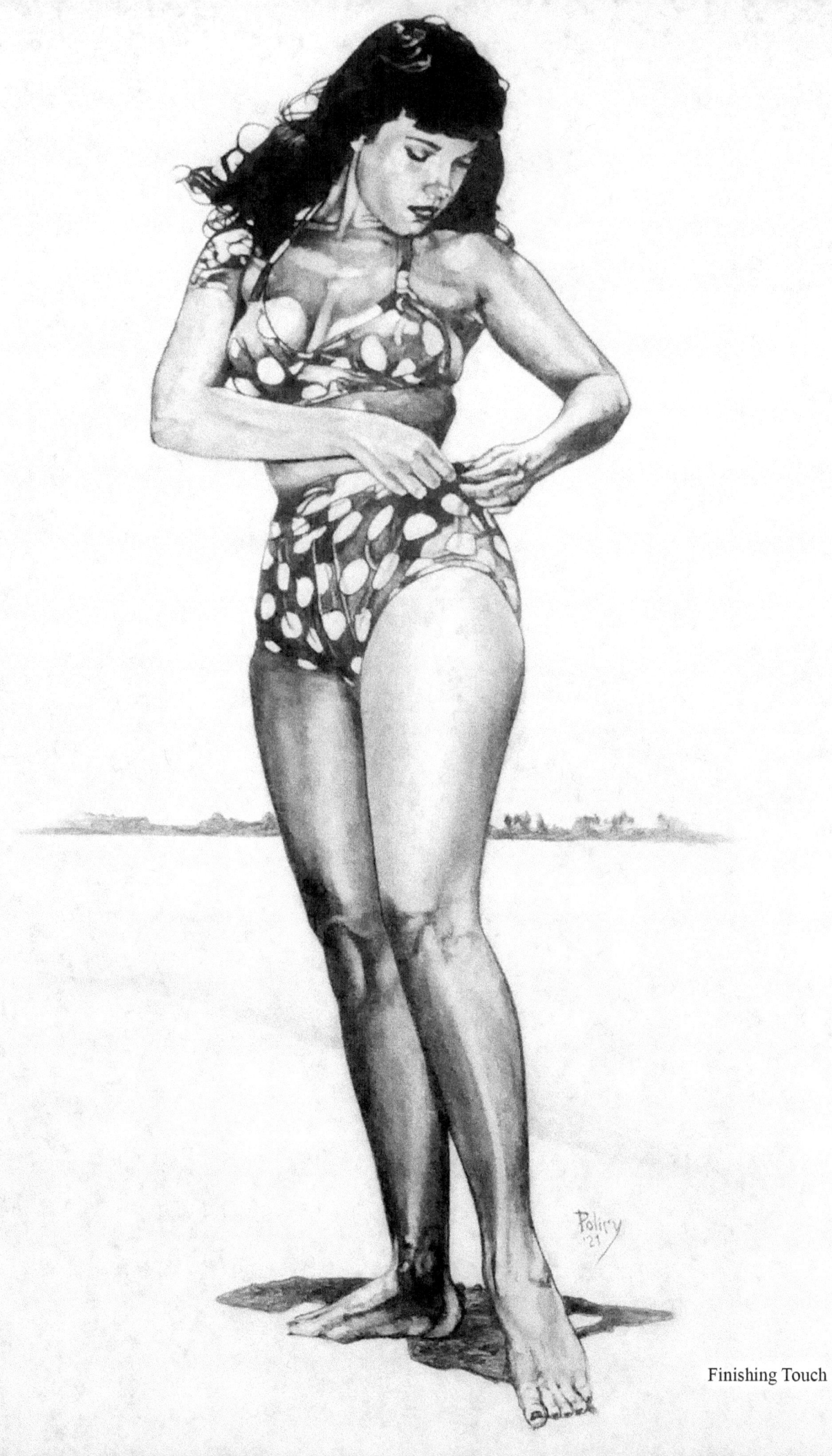

Finishing Touch

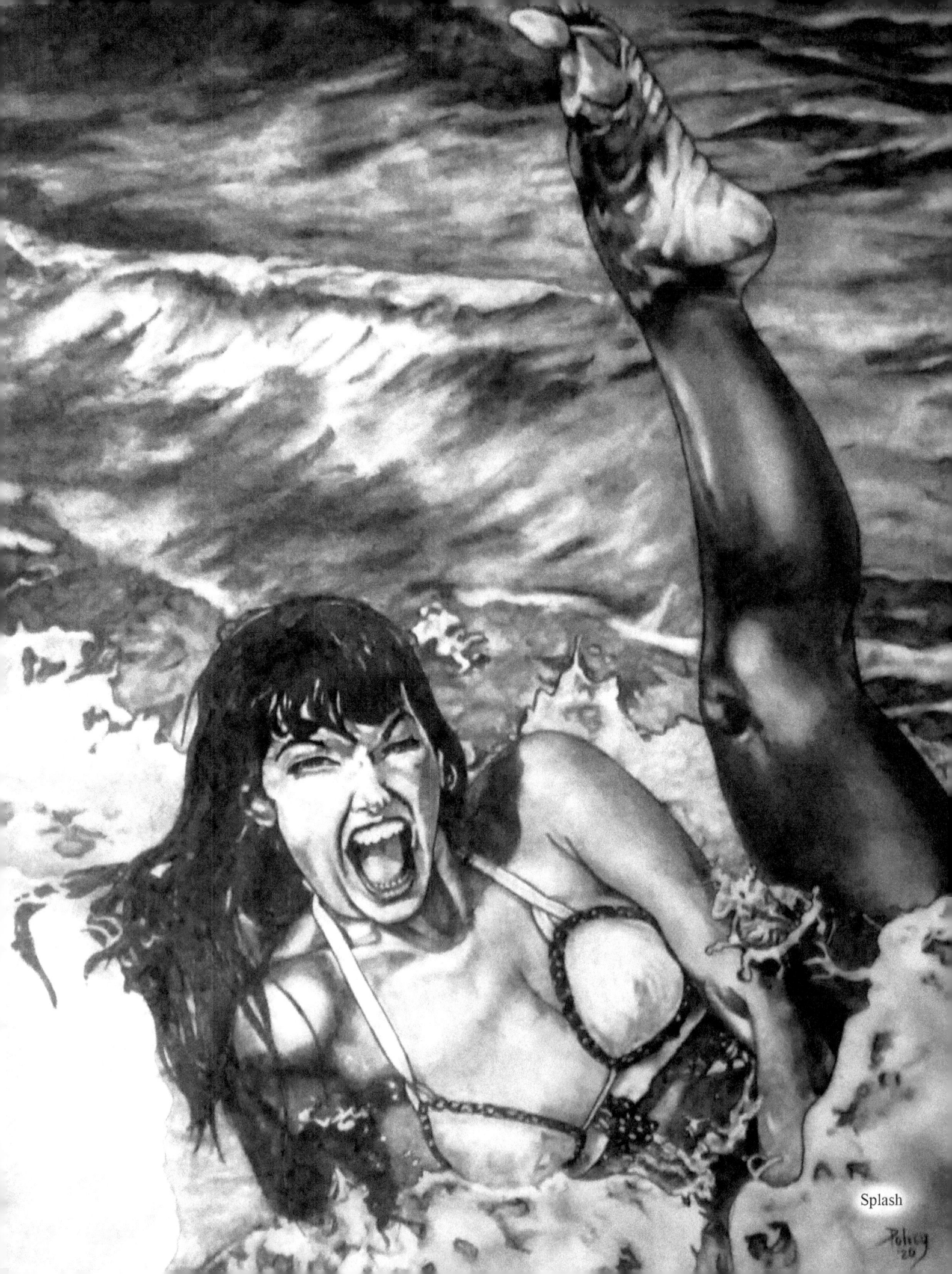
Splash

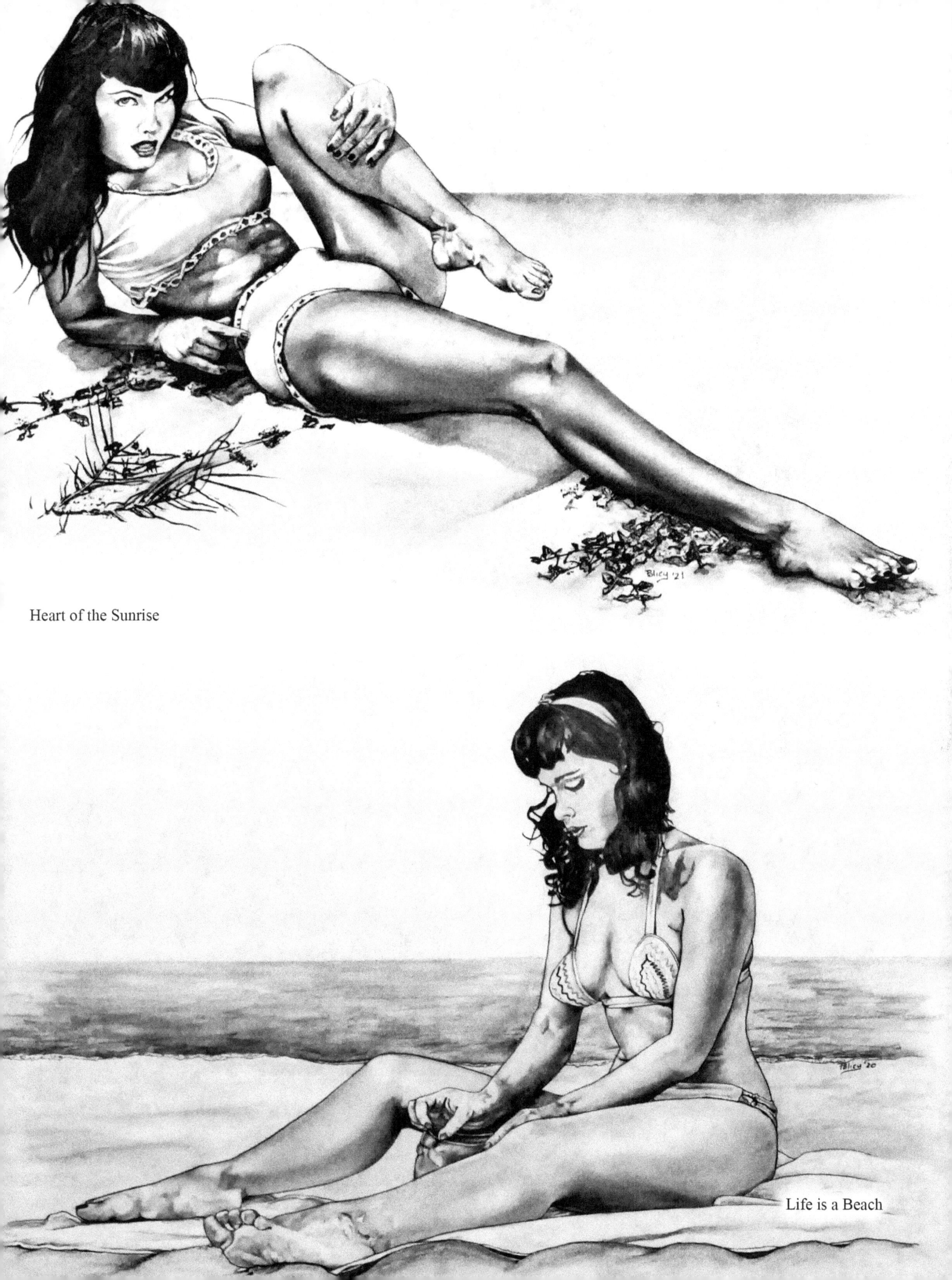

Heart of the Sunrise

Life is a Beach

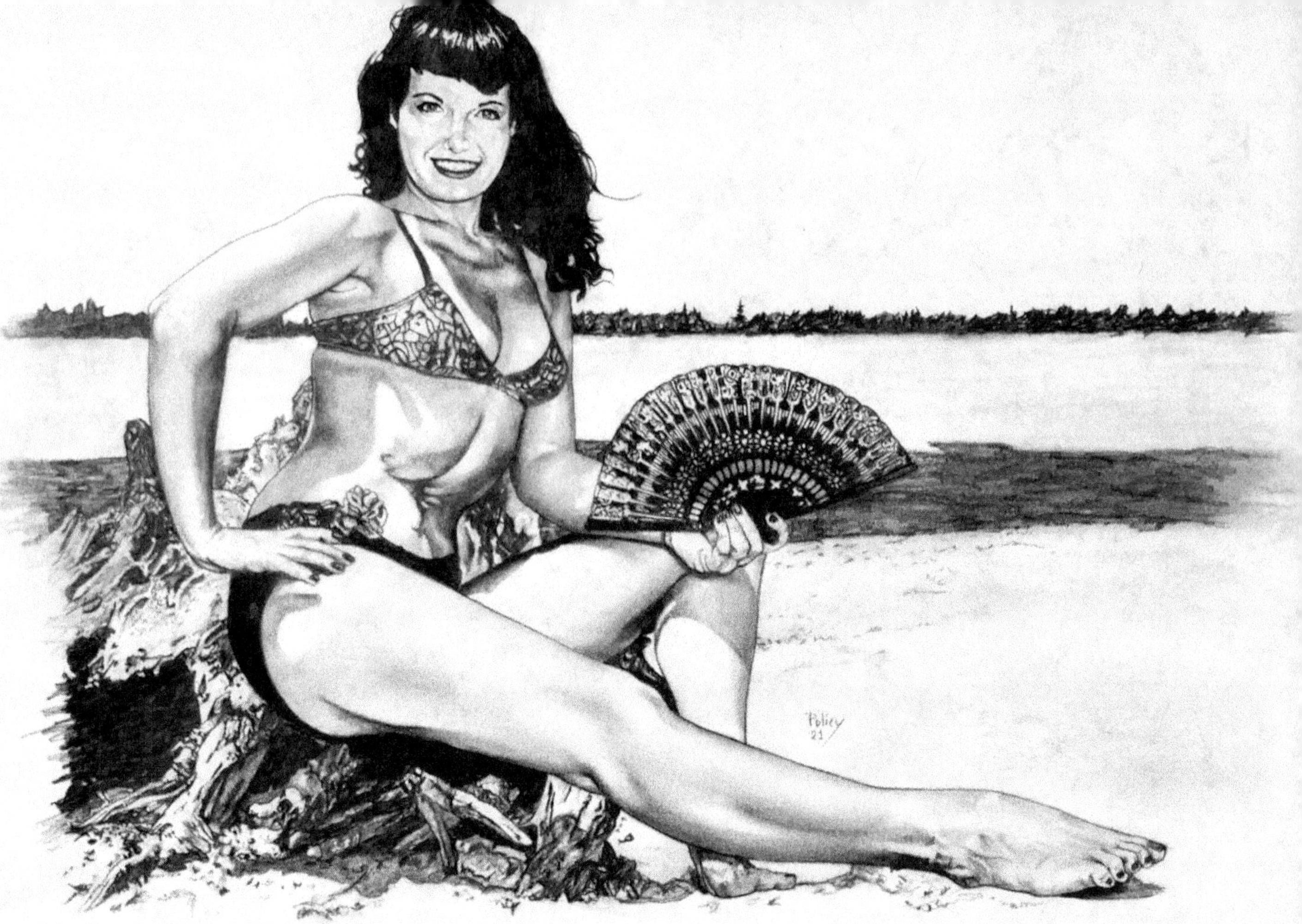

Big Fan of the Beach

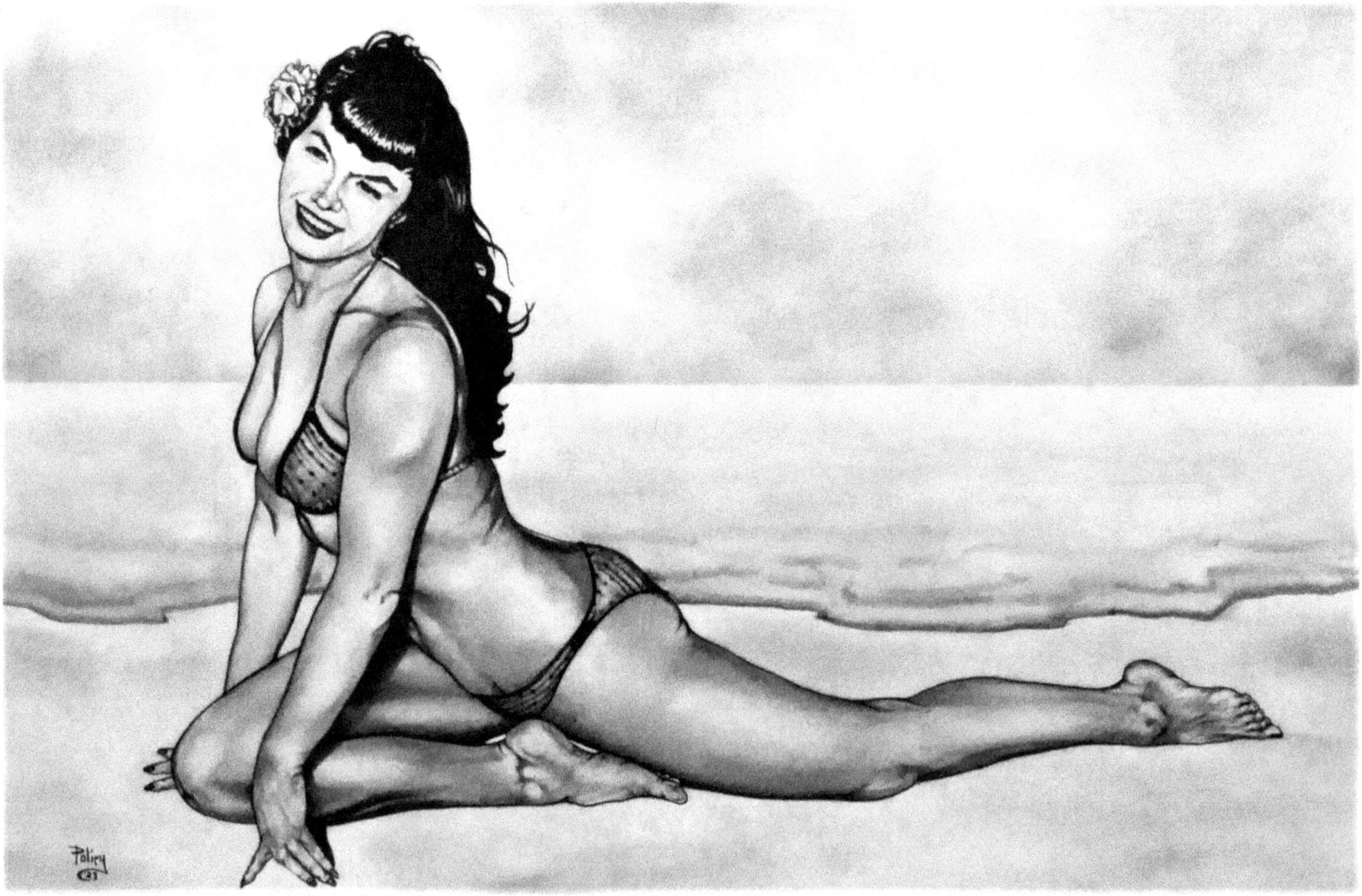

Nice ... Flower

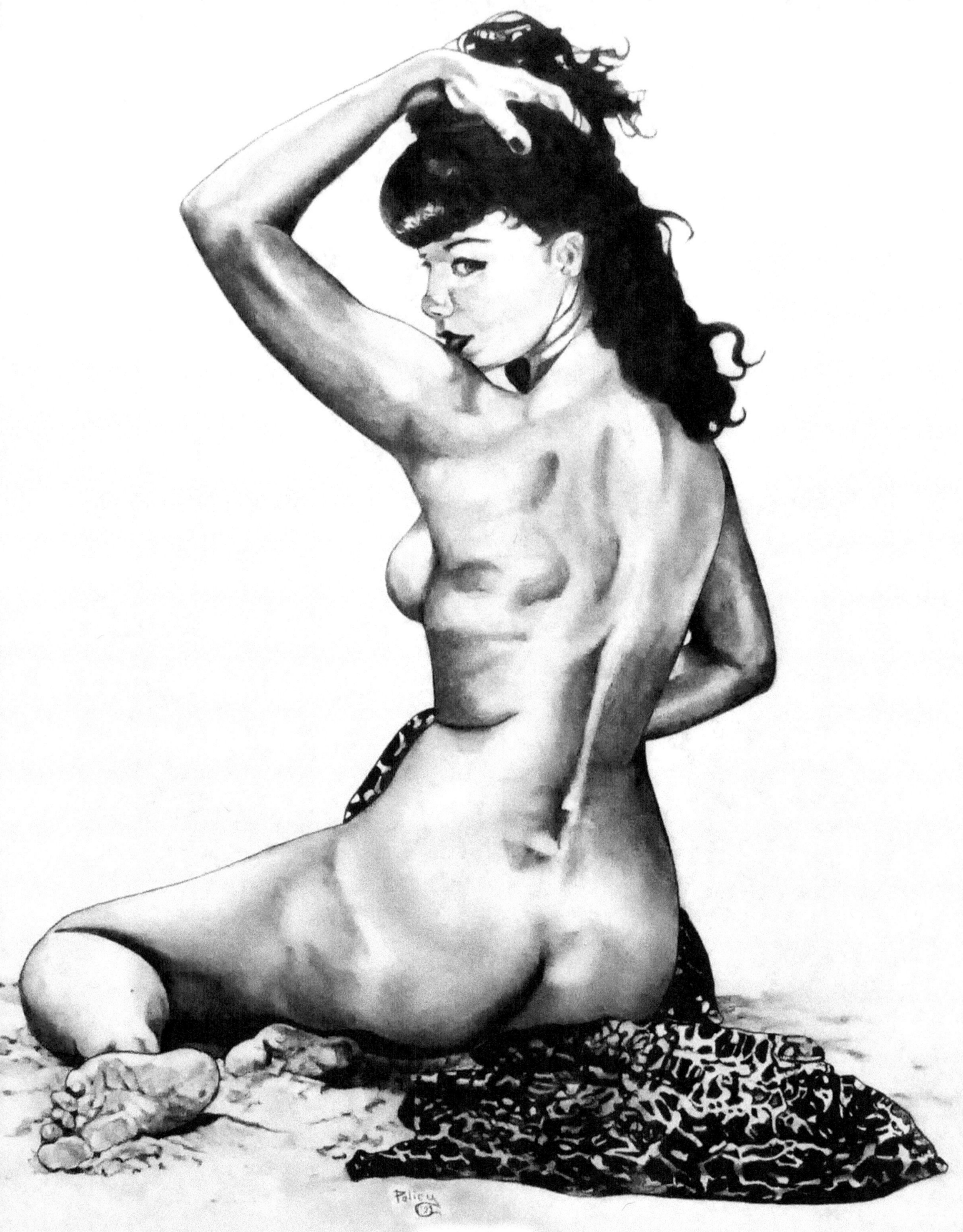

Pause and Reflect

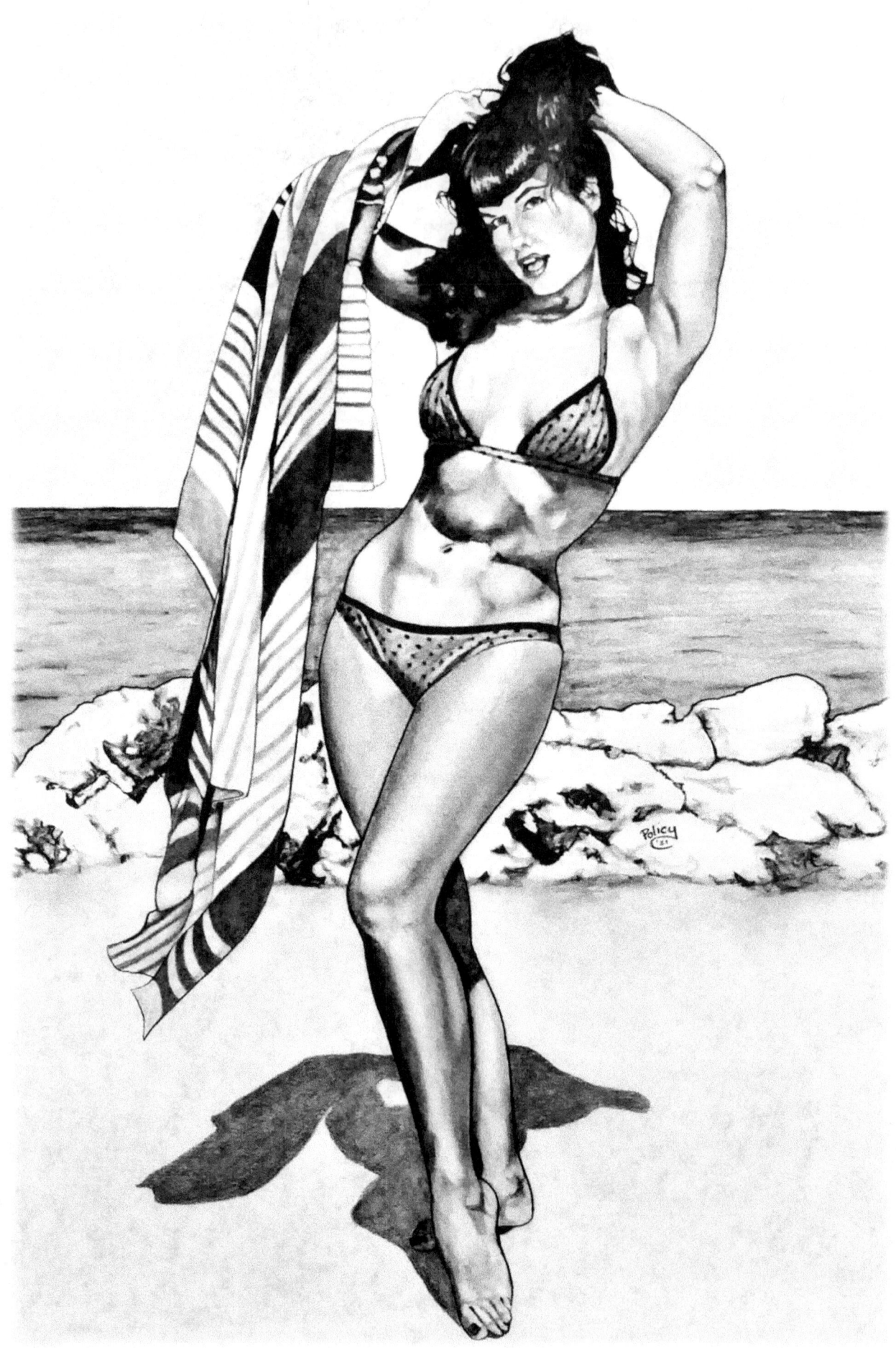

Nice ... Beach Towel

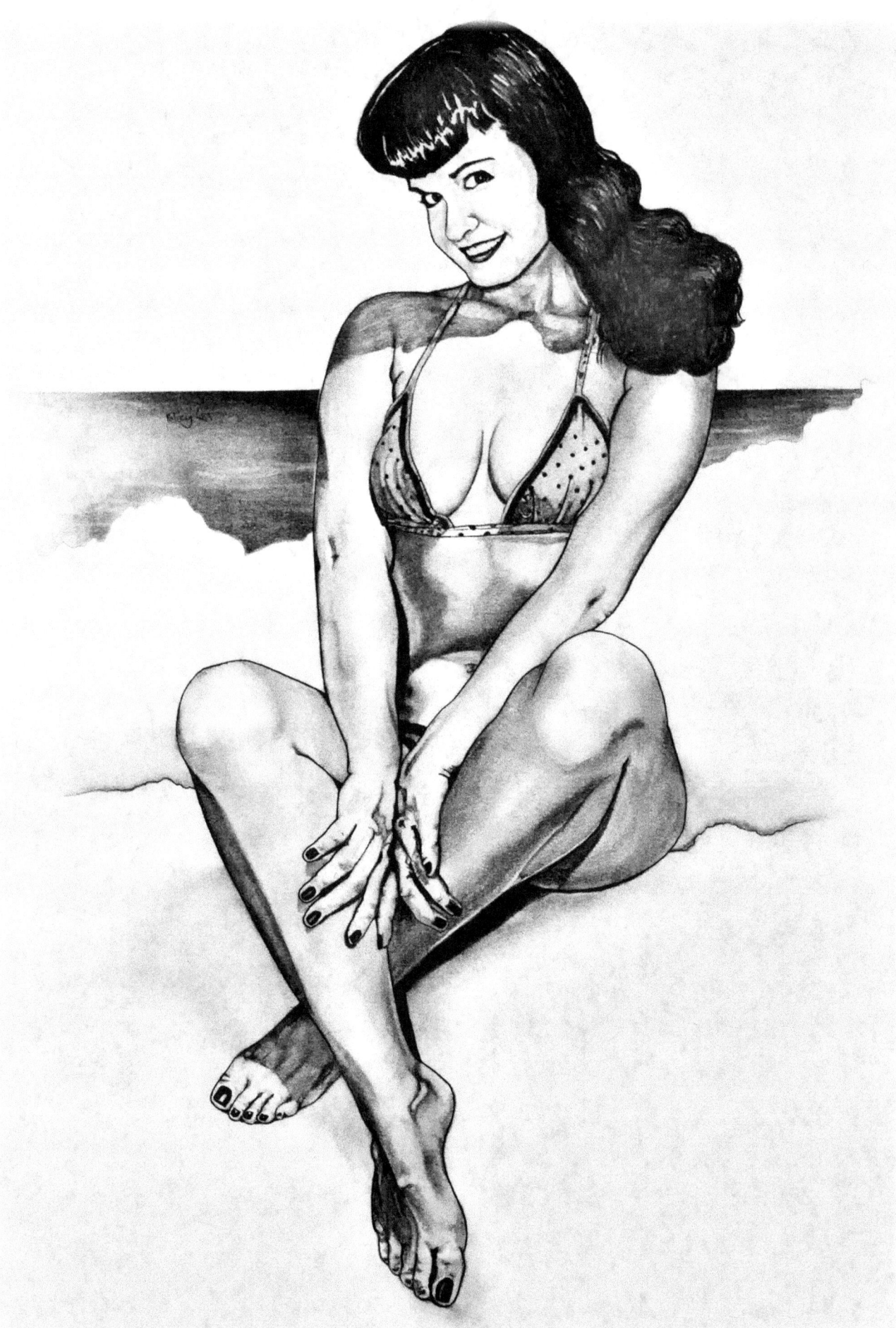

Smile

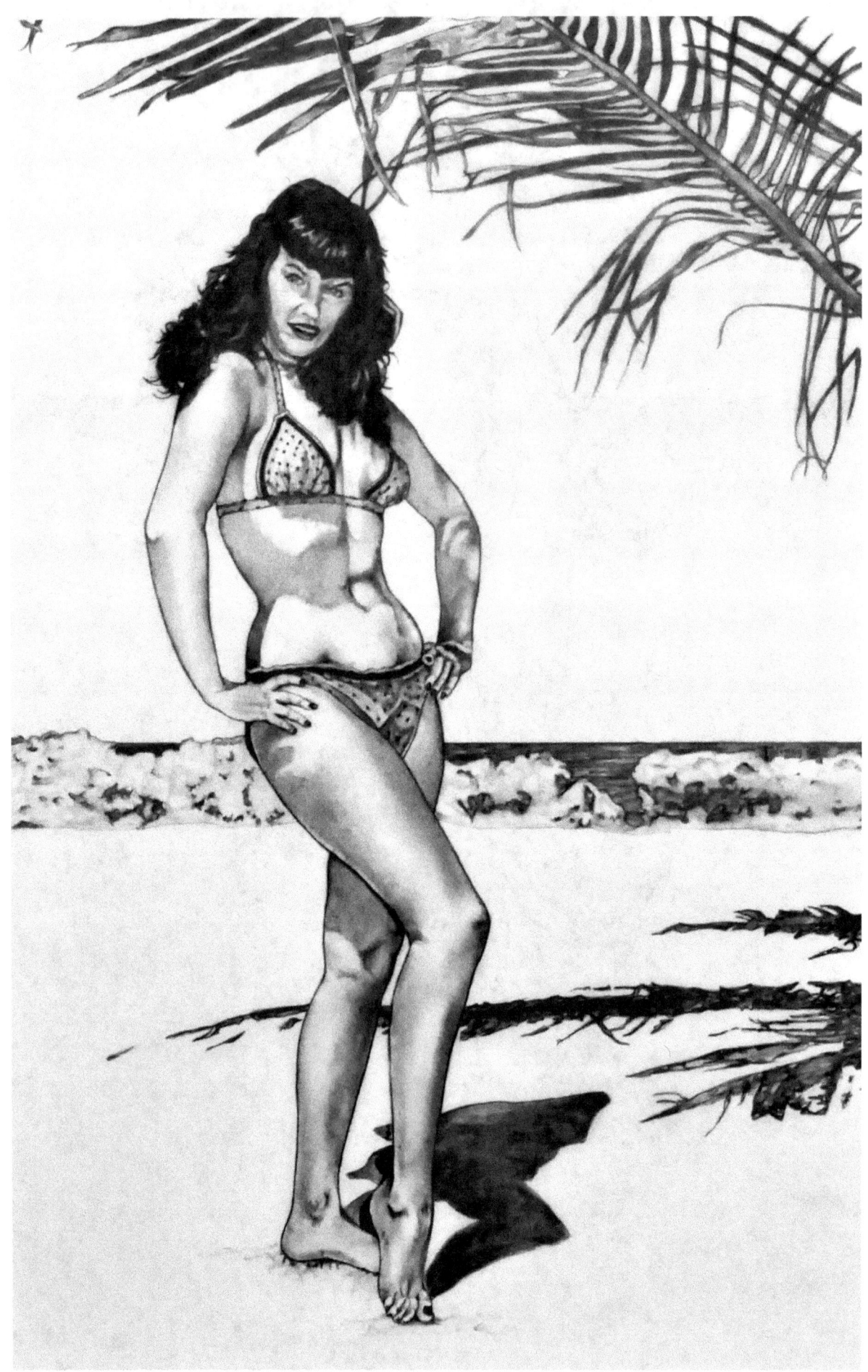

It's Sunny Somewhere

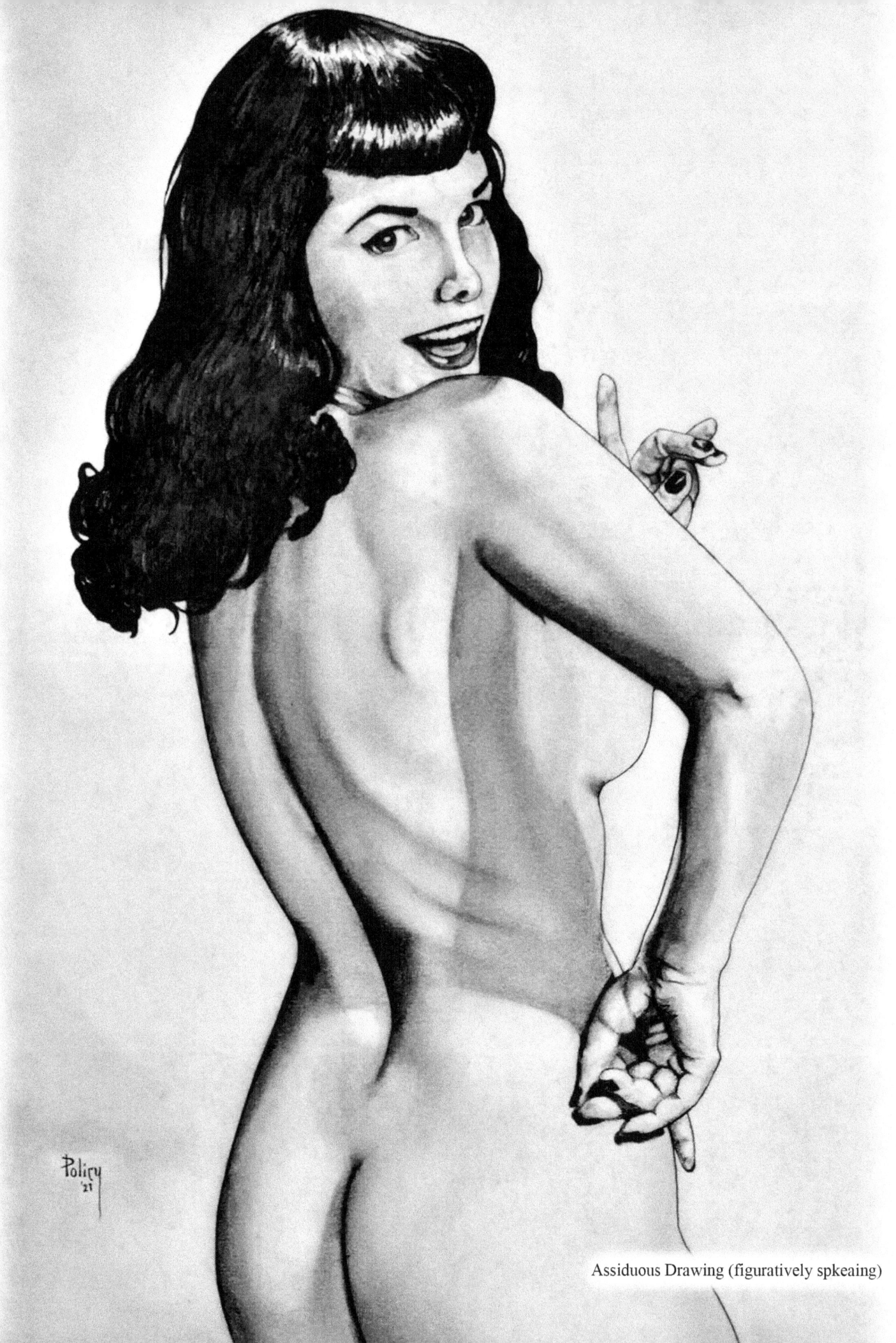

Assiduous Drawing (figuratively spkeaing)

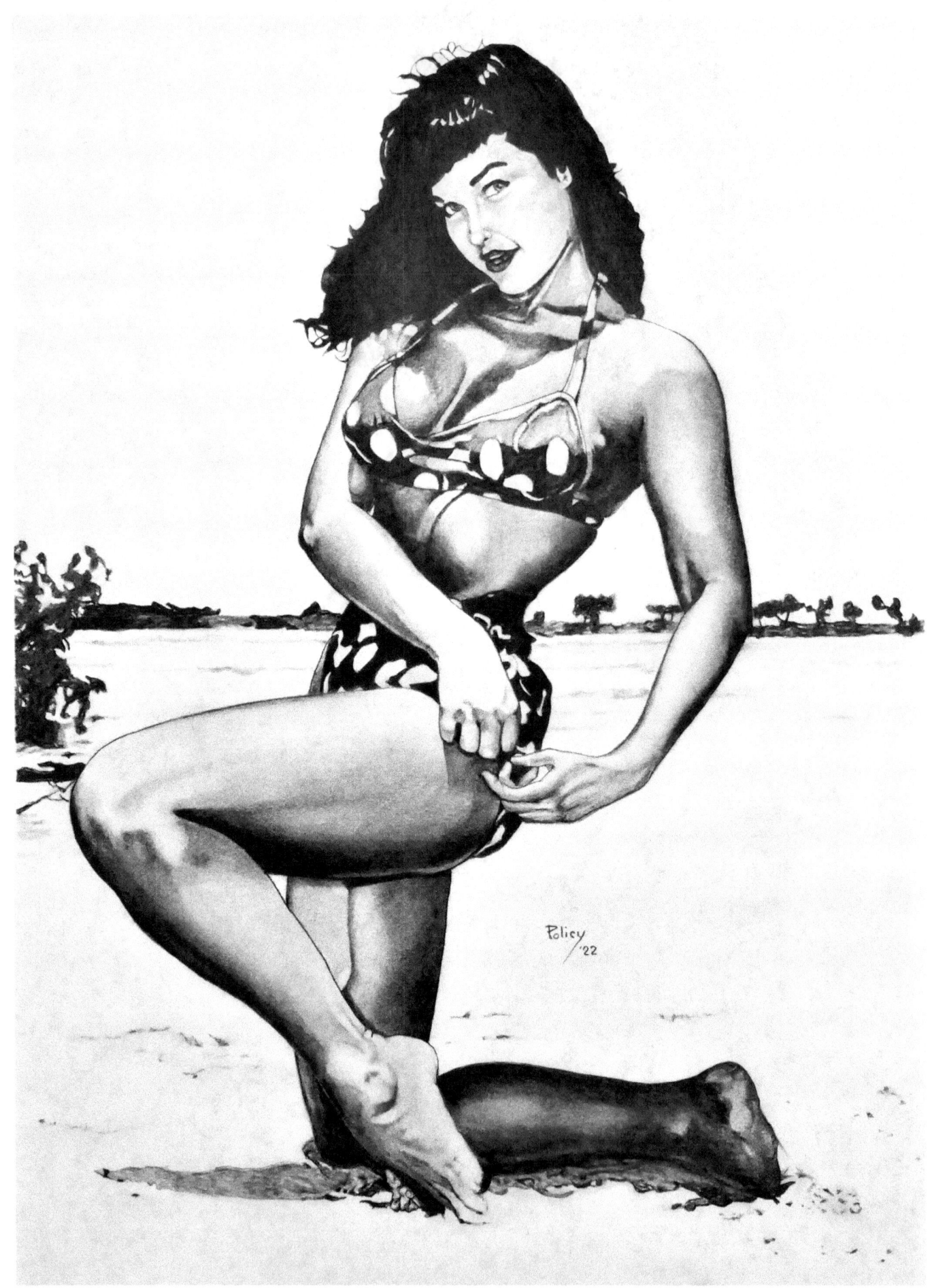

A Little Help

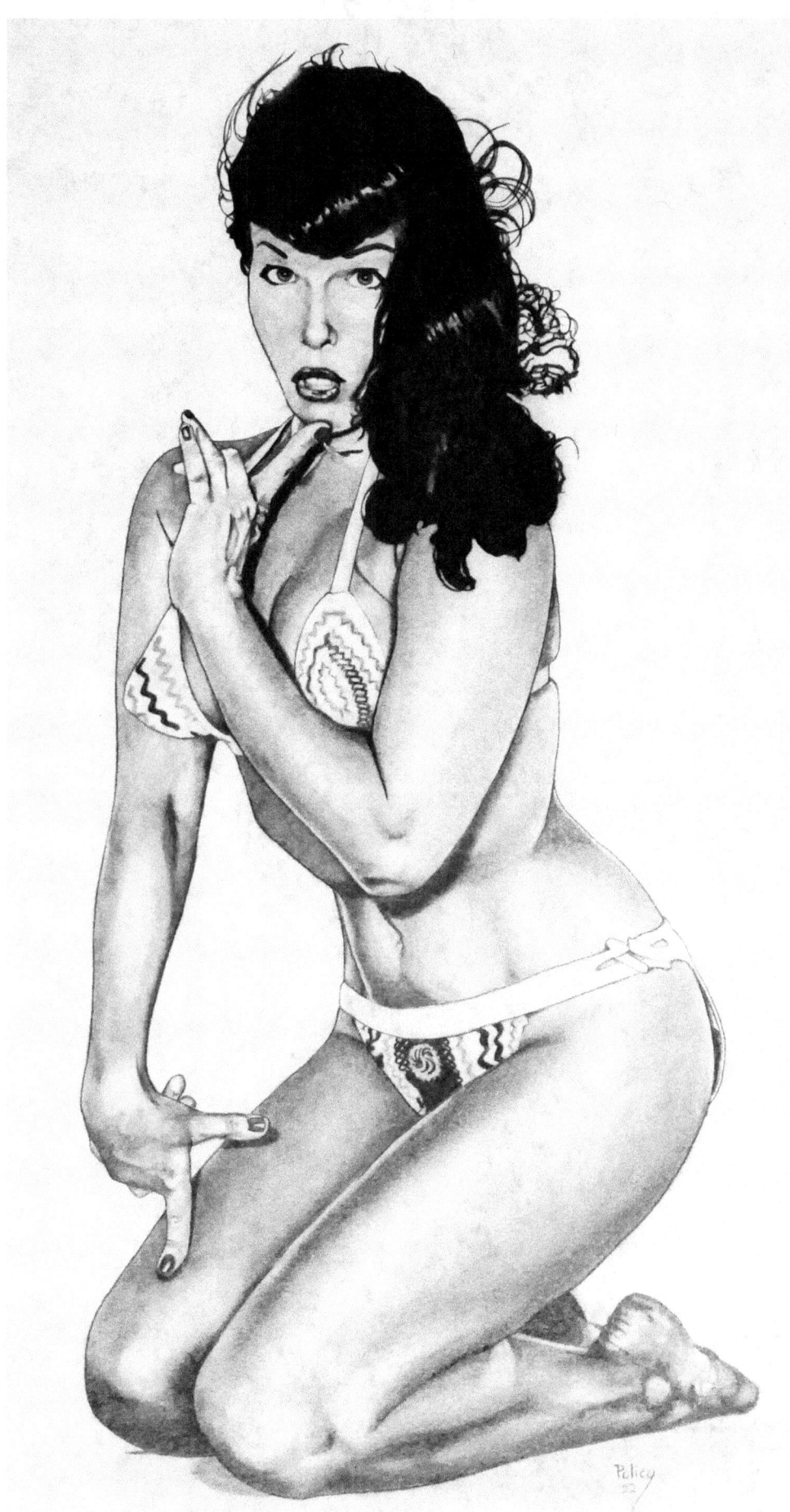

Hello Boys

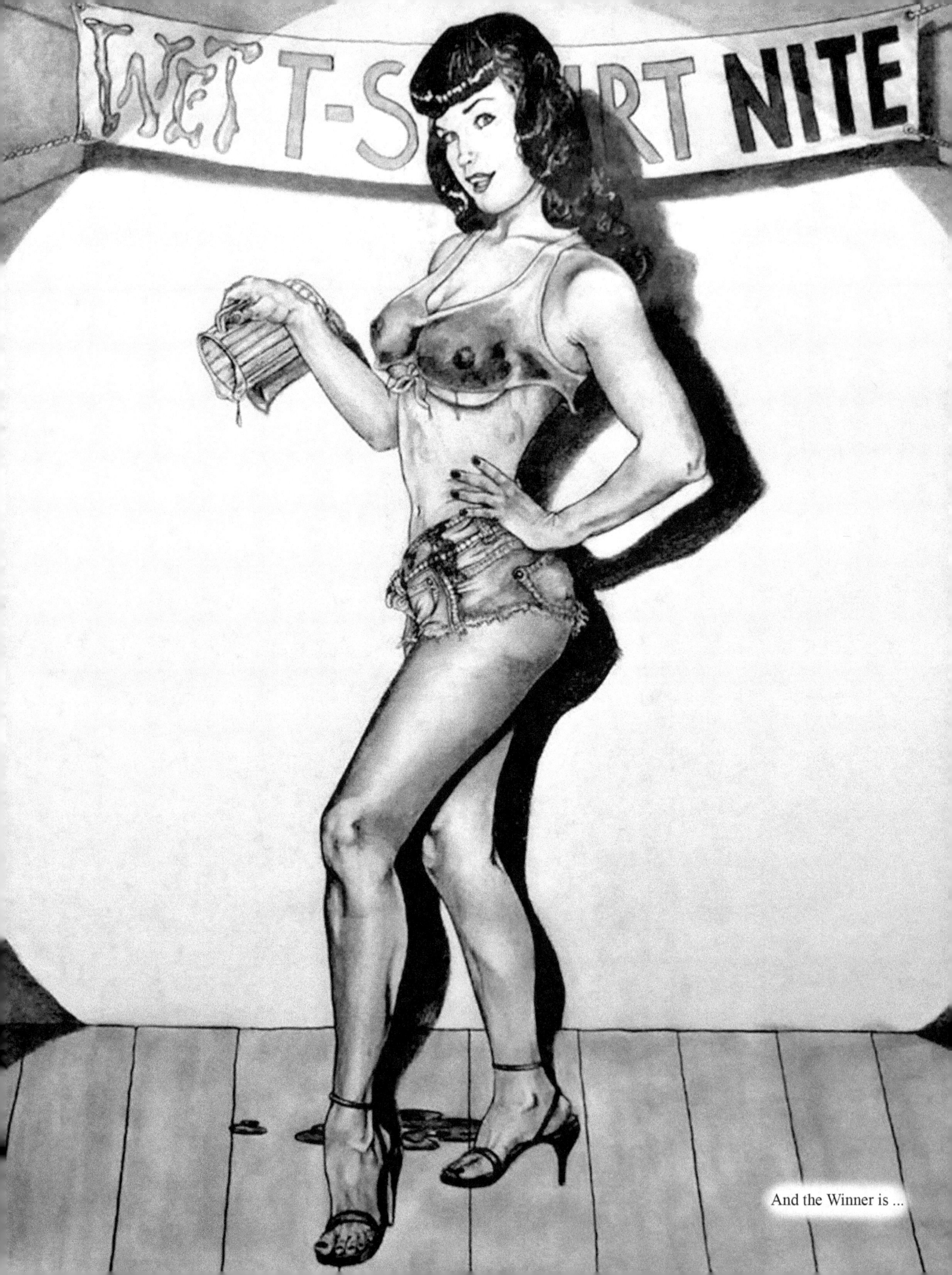

And the Winner is ...

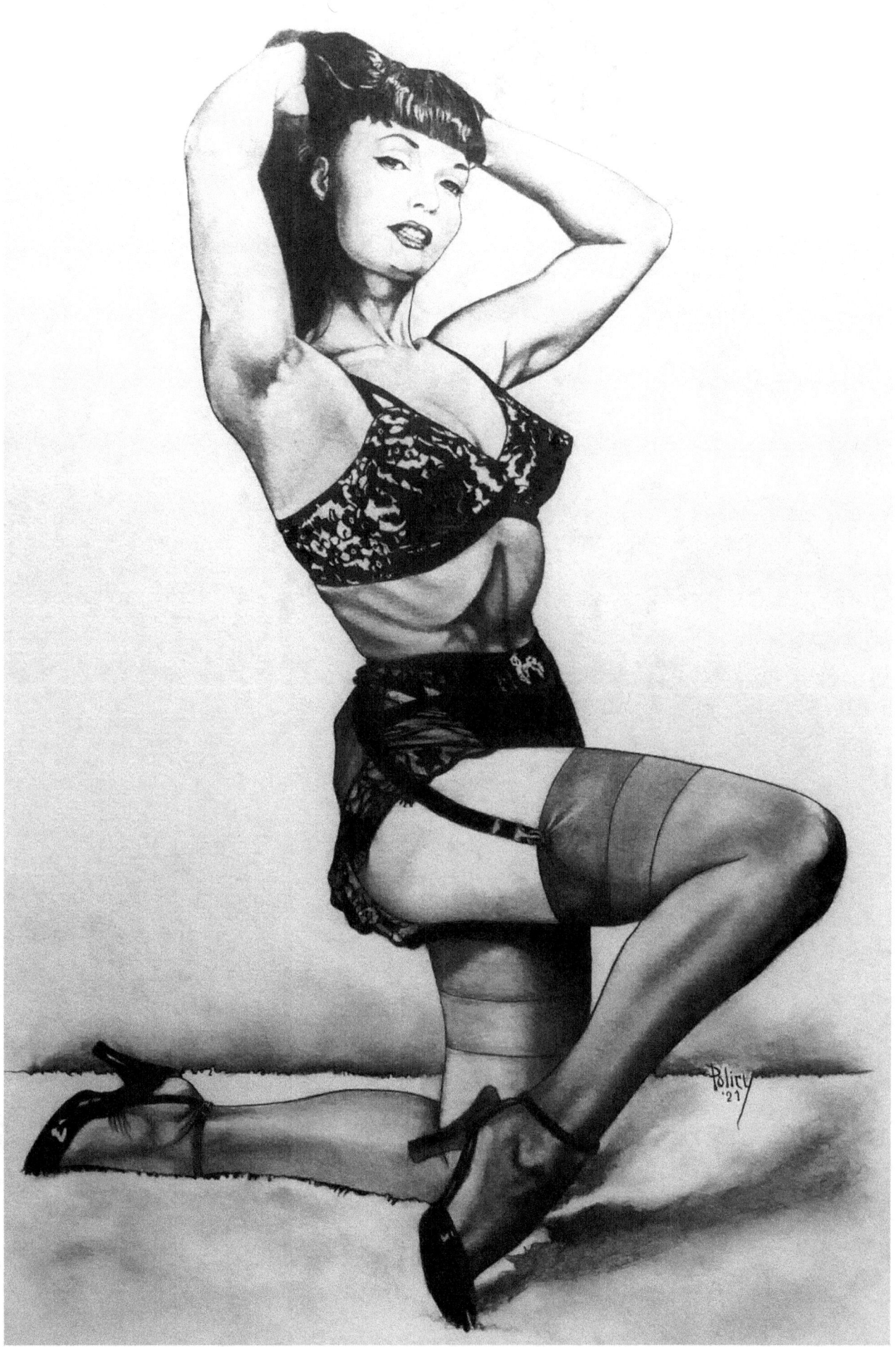

Shy Heels

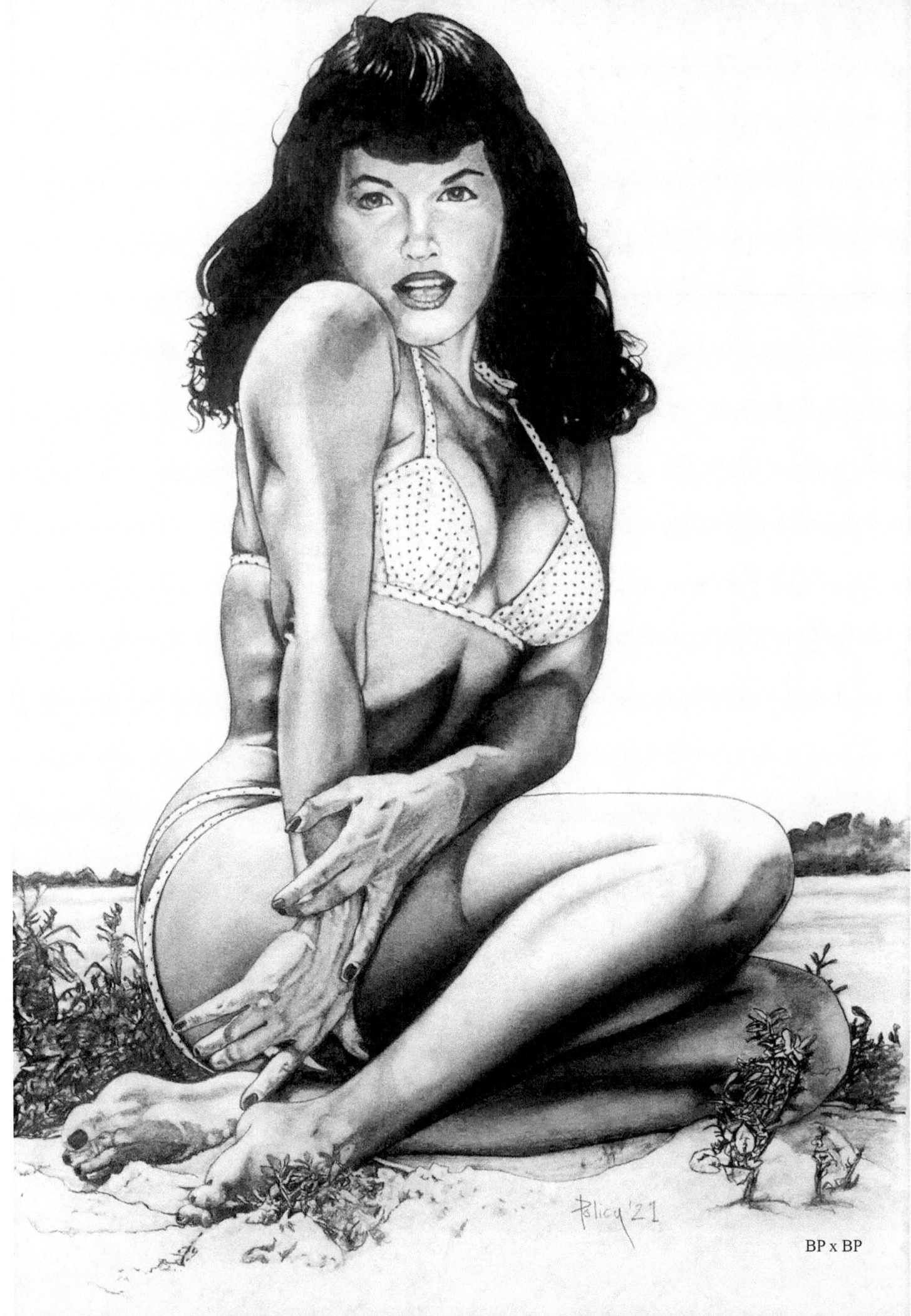

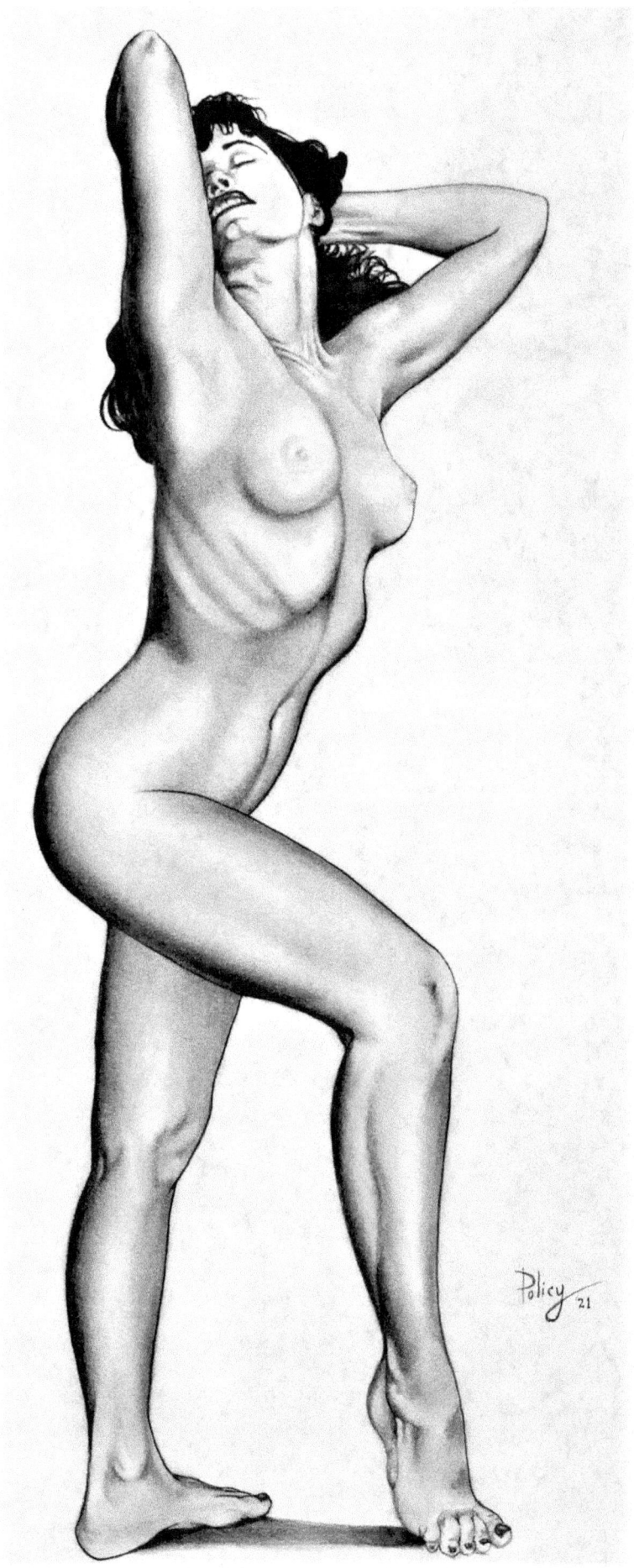

Standing Room Only

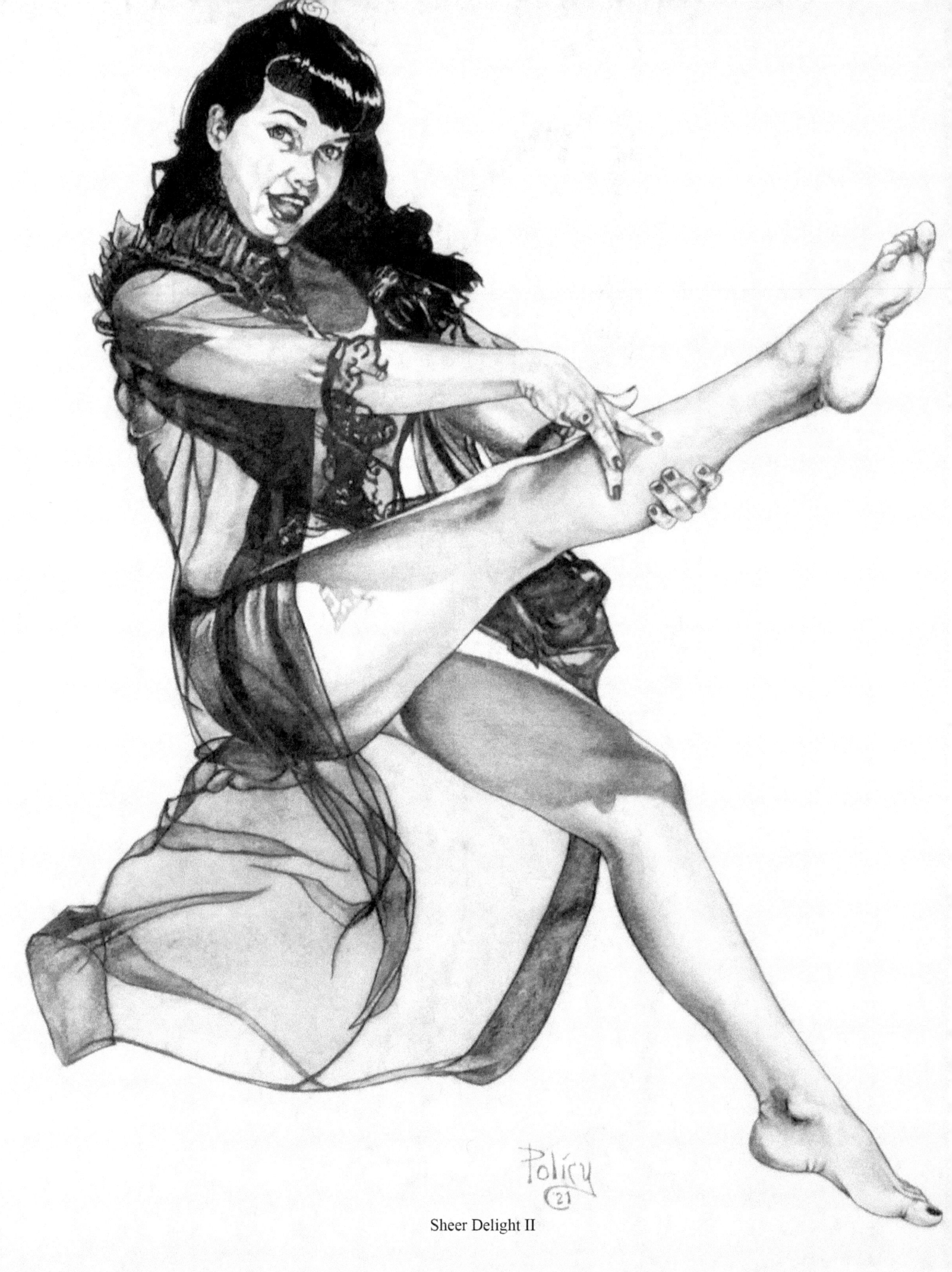

Sheer Delight II

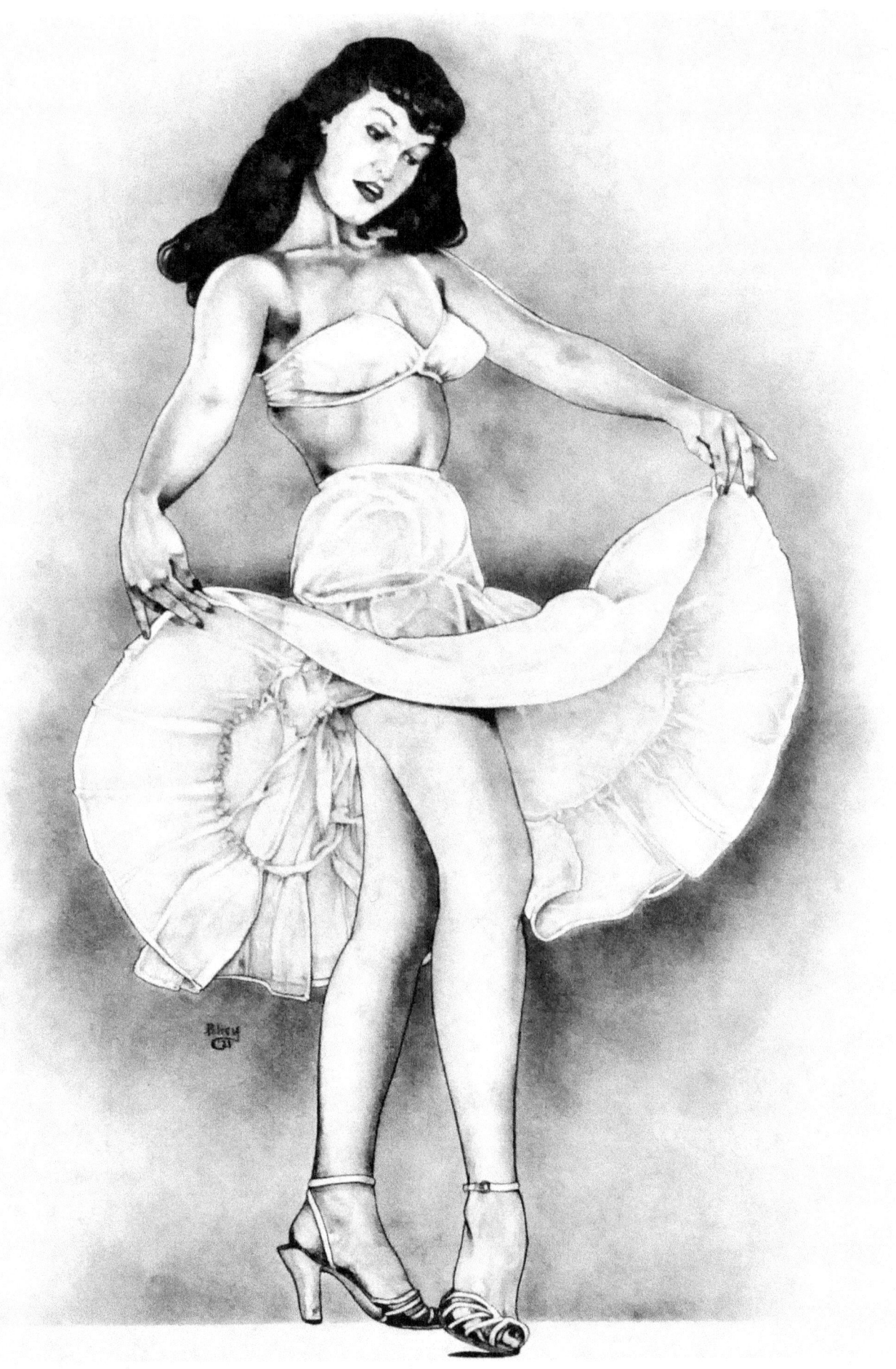

Skirting ... The Issue

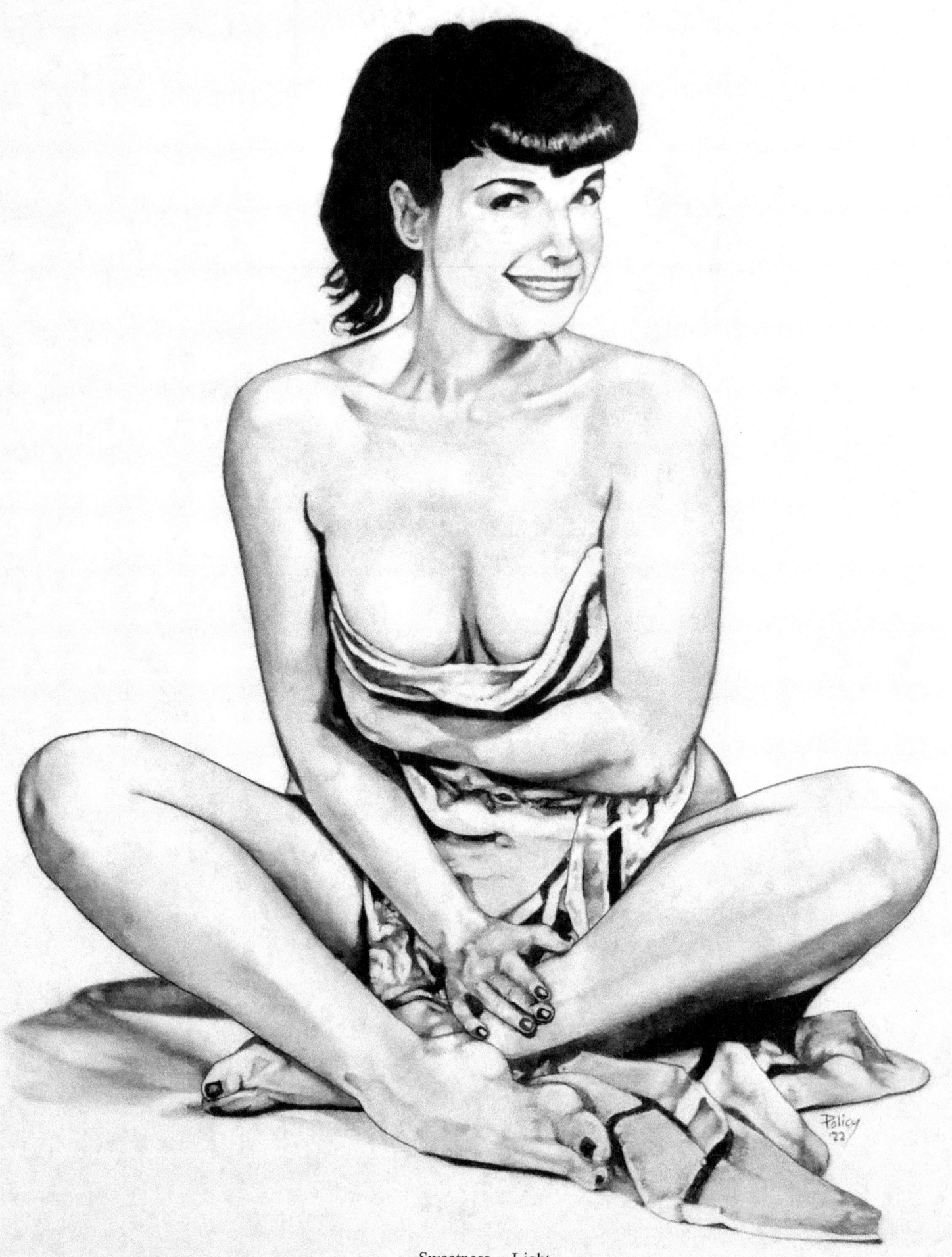

Sweetness ... Light

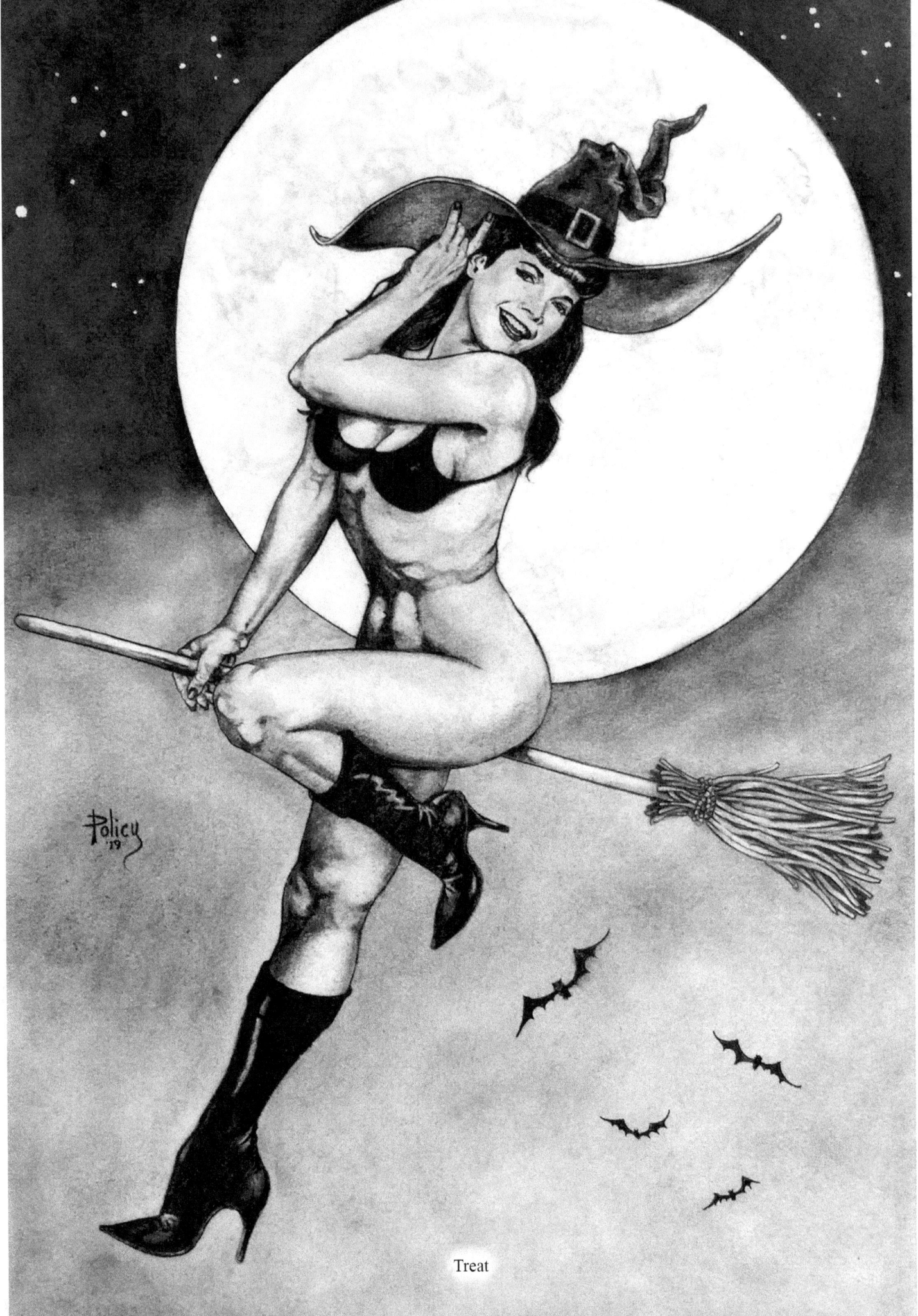

Treat

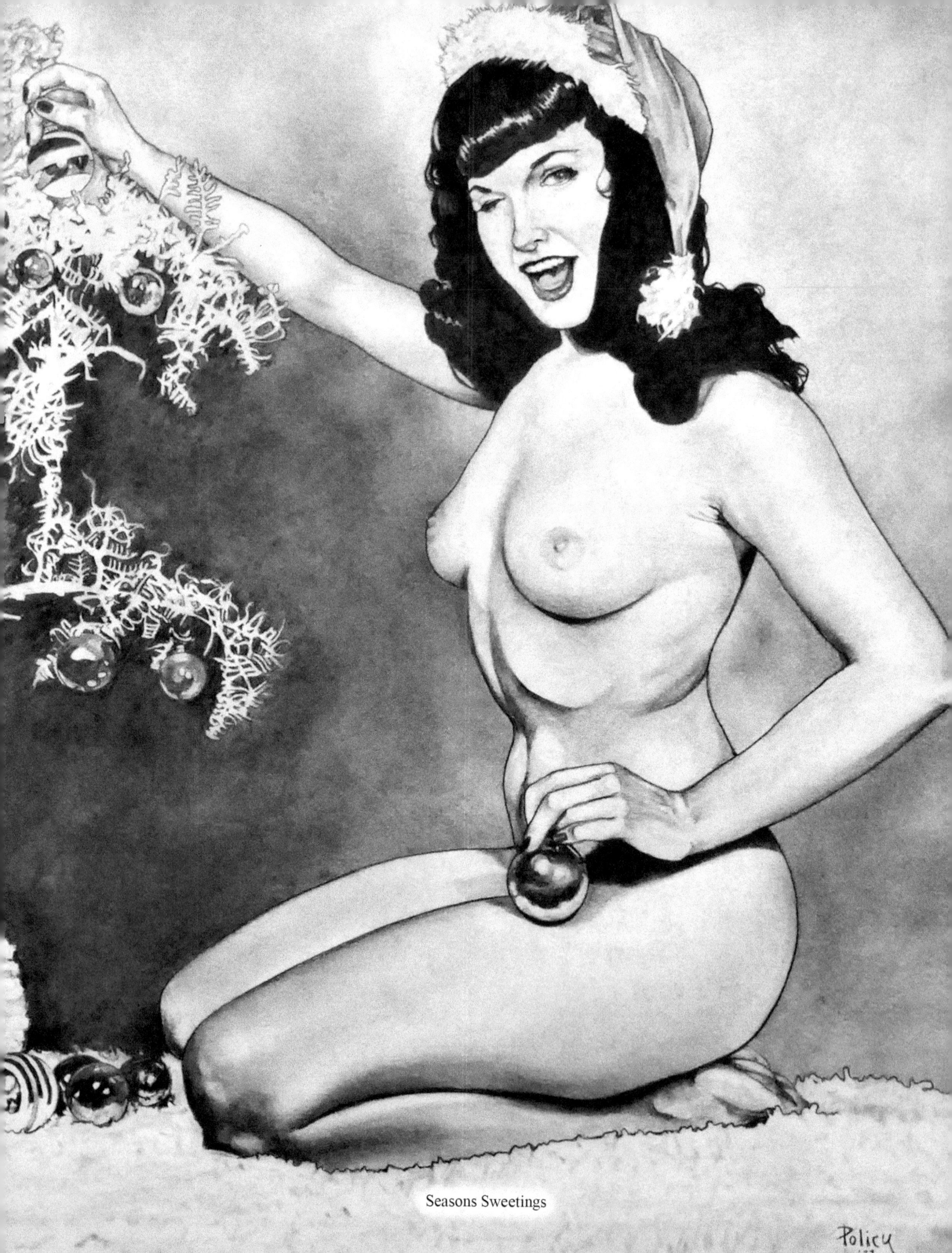
Seasons Sweetings

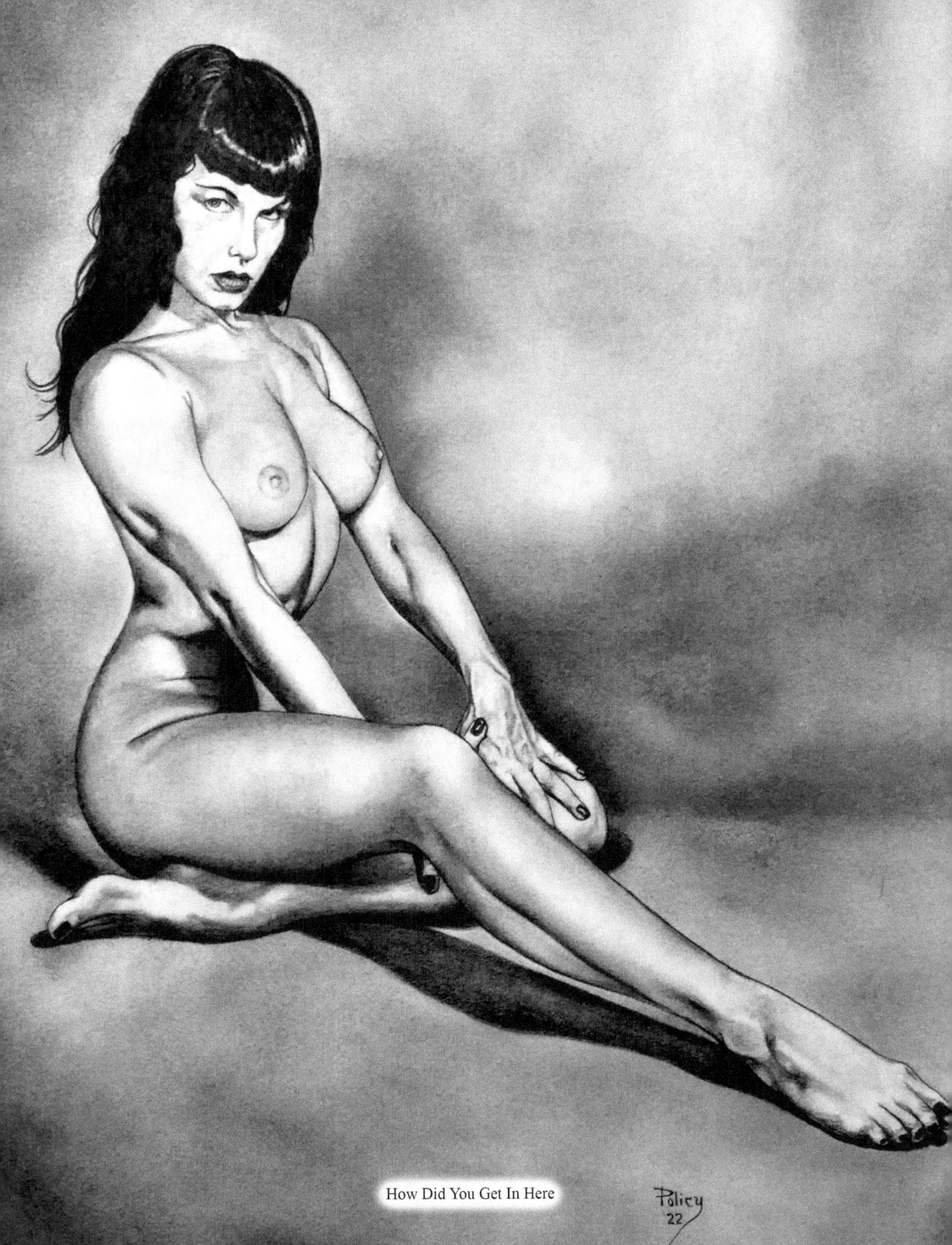

How Did You Get In Here

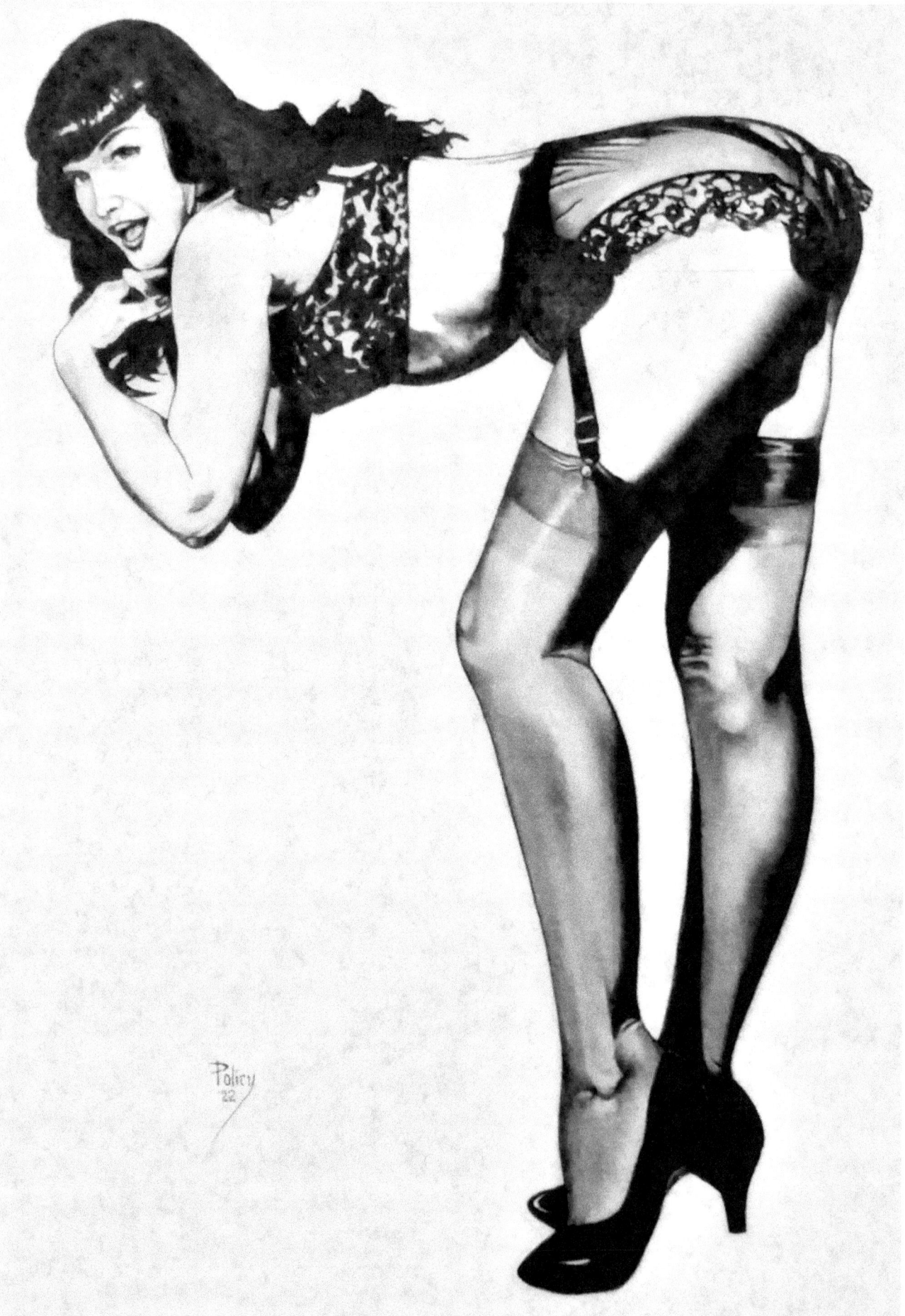

Lean

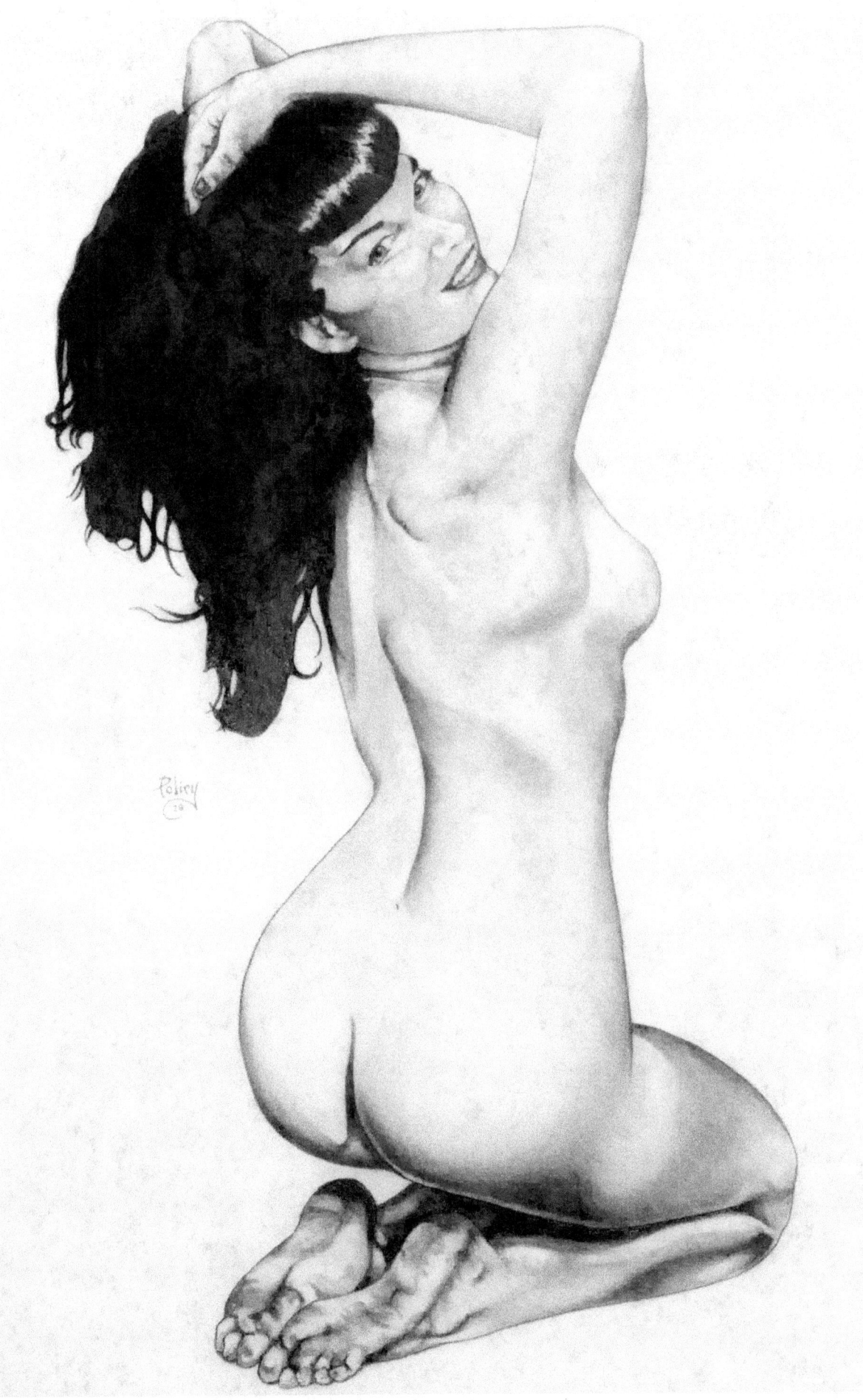

But ...

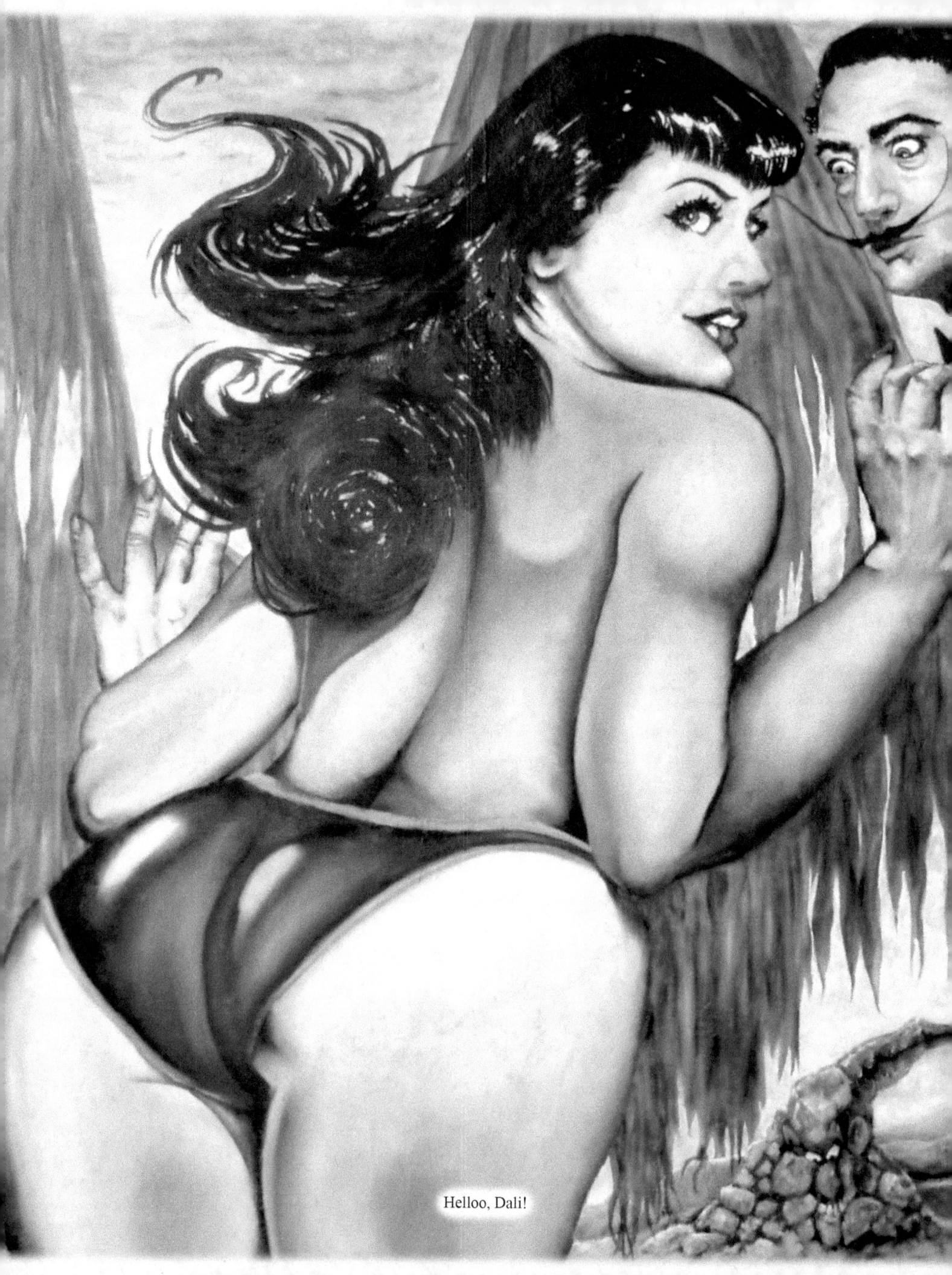
Helloo, Dali!

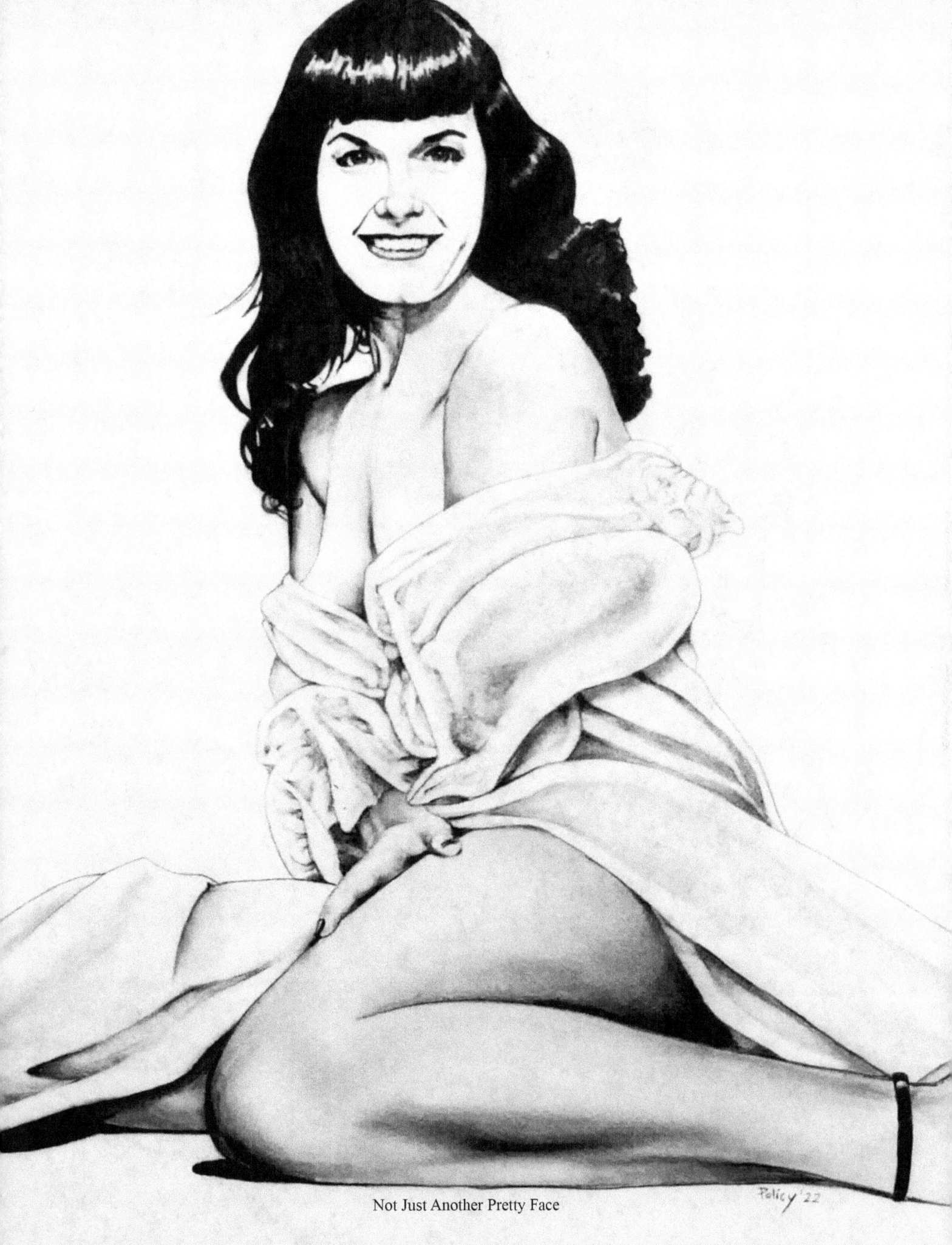

Not Just Another Pretty Face

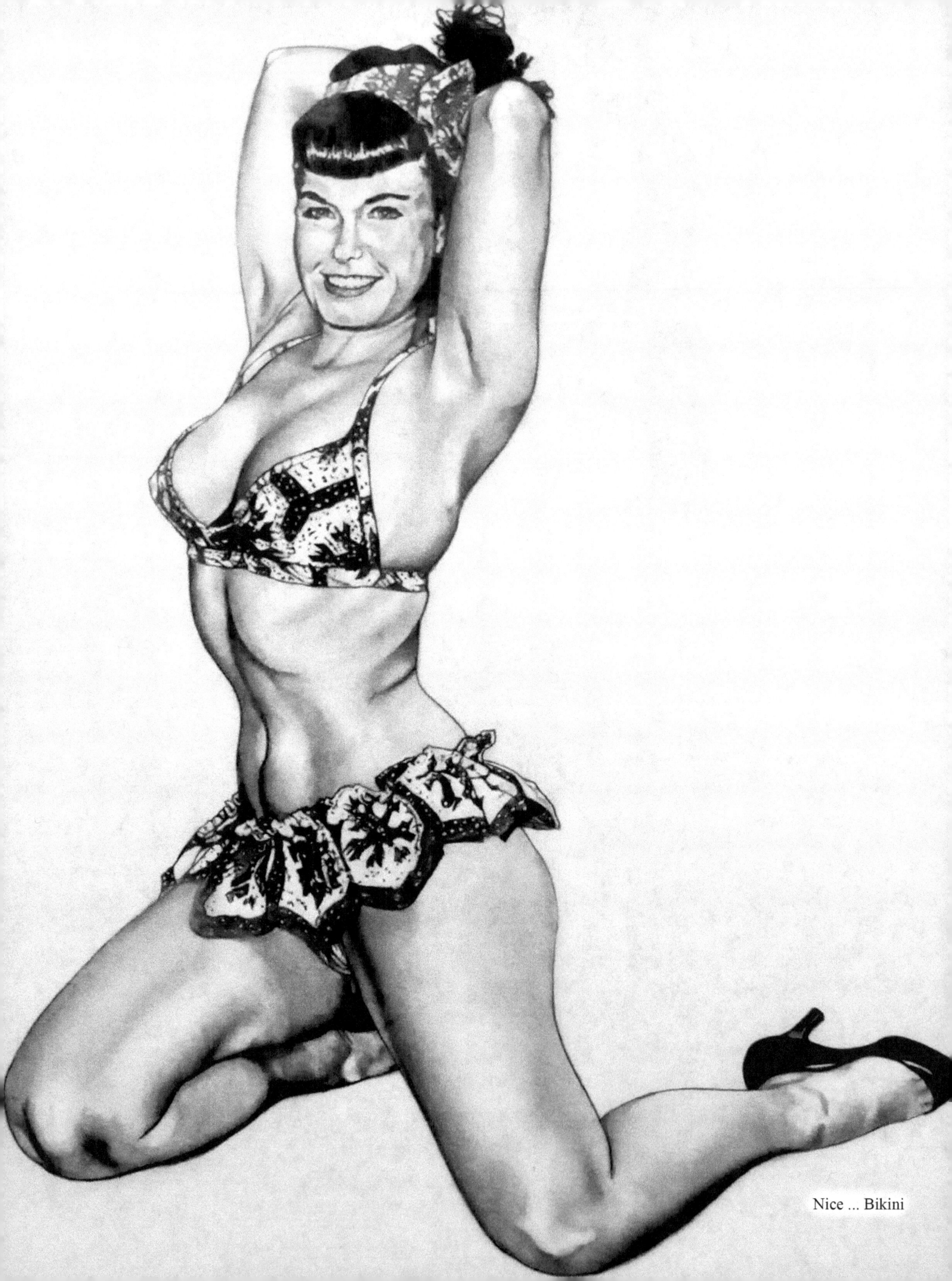

Nice ... Bikini

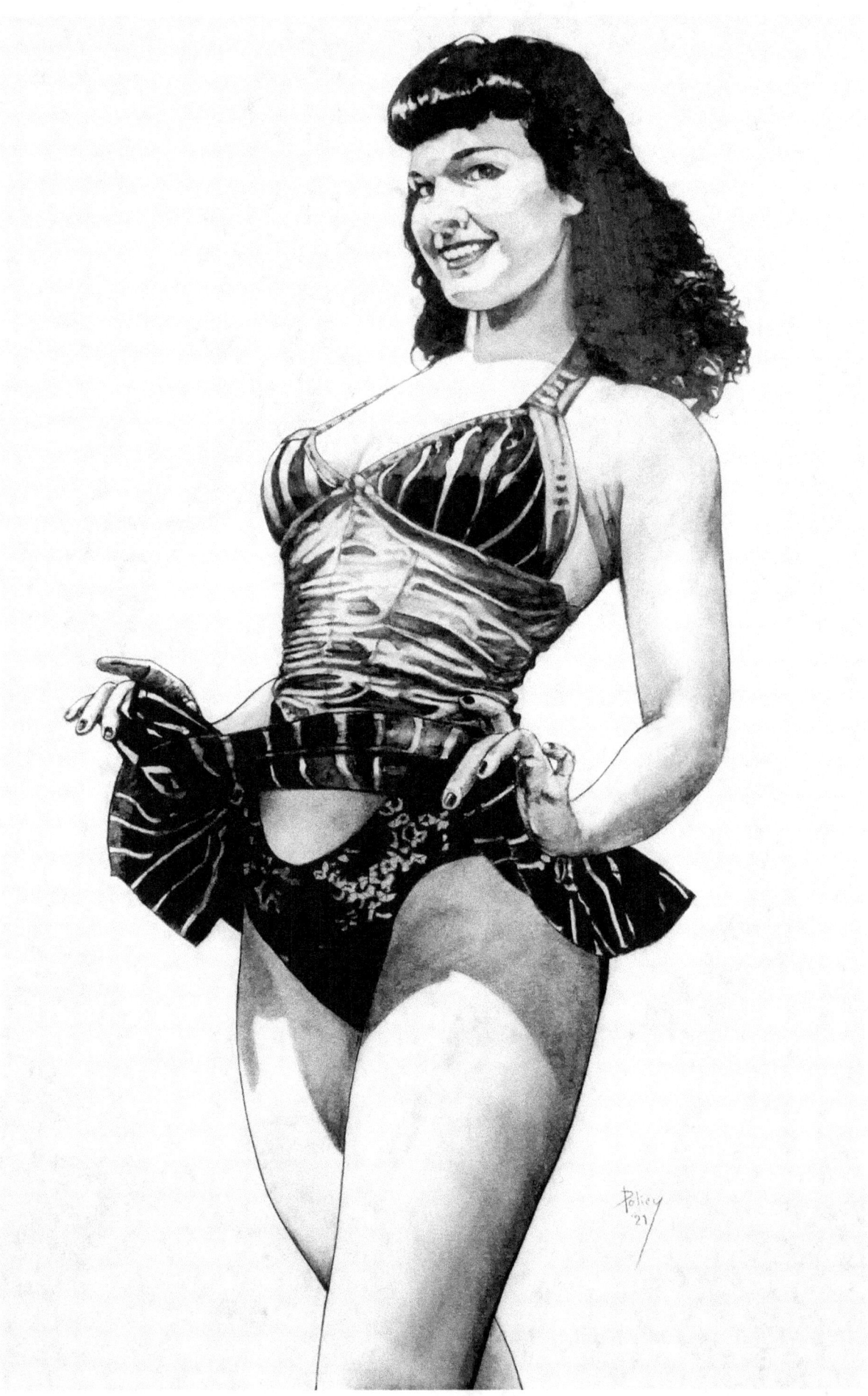

Summer Breeze

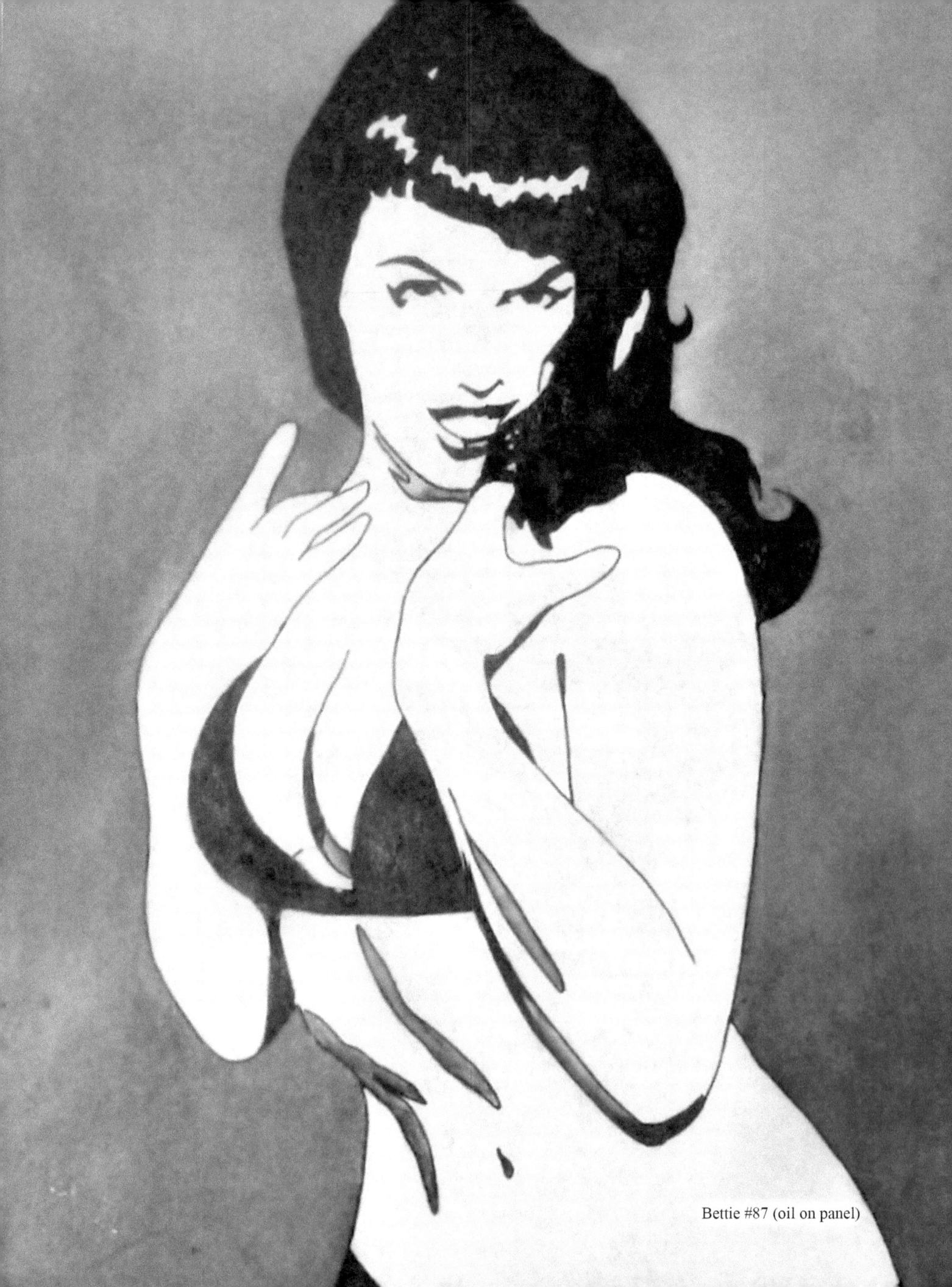

Bettie #87 (oil on panel)

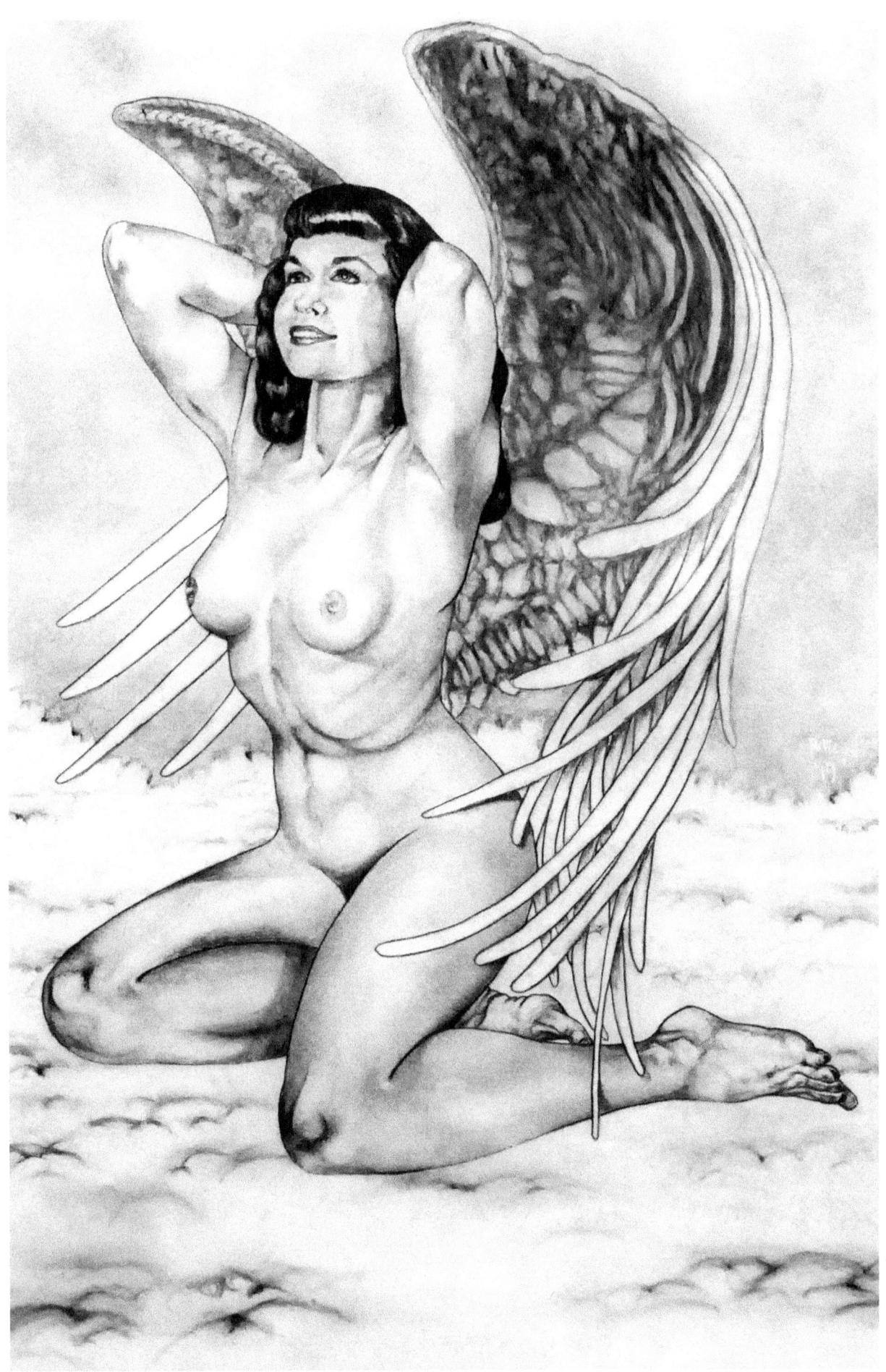

Heavenly Body

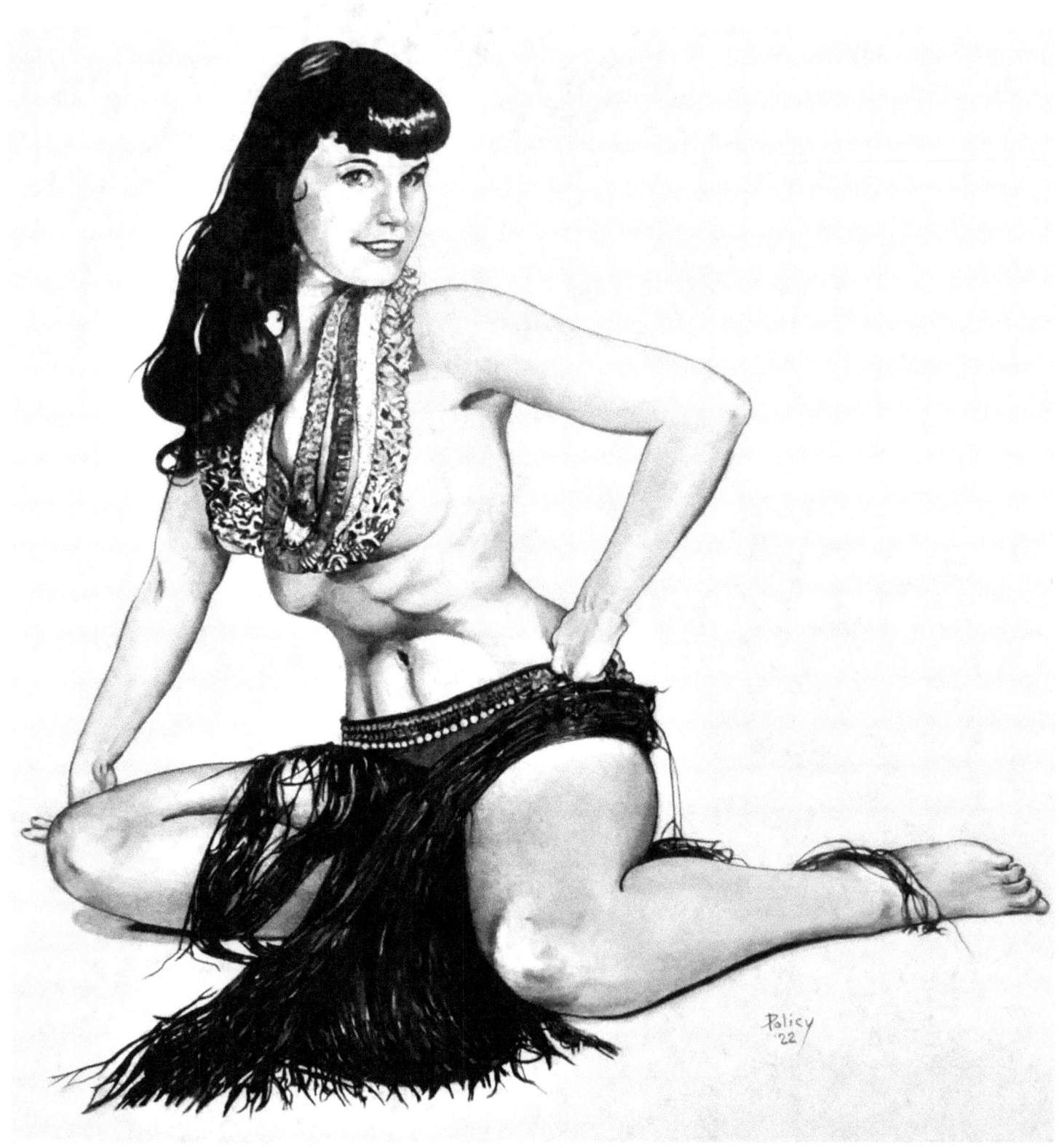

Just Got Leid

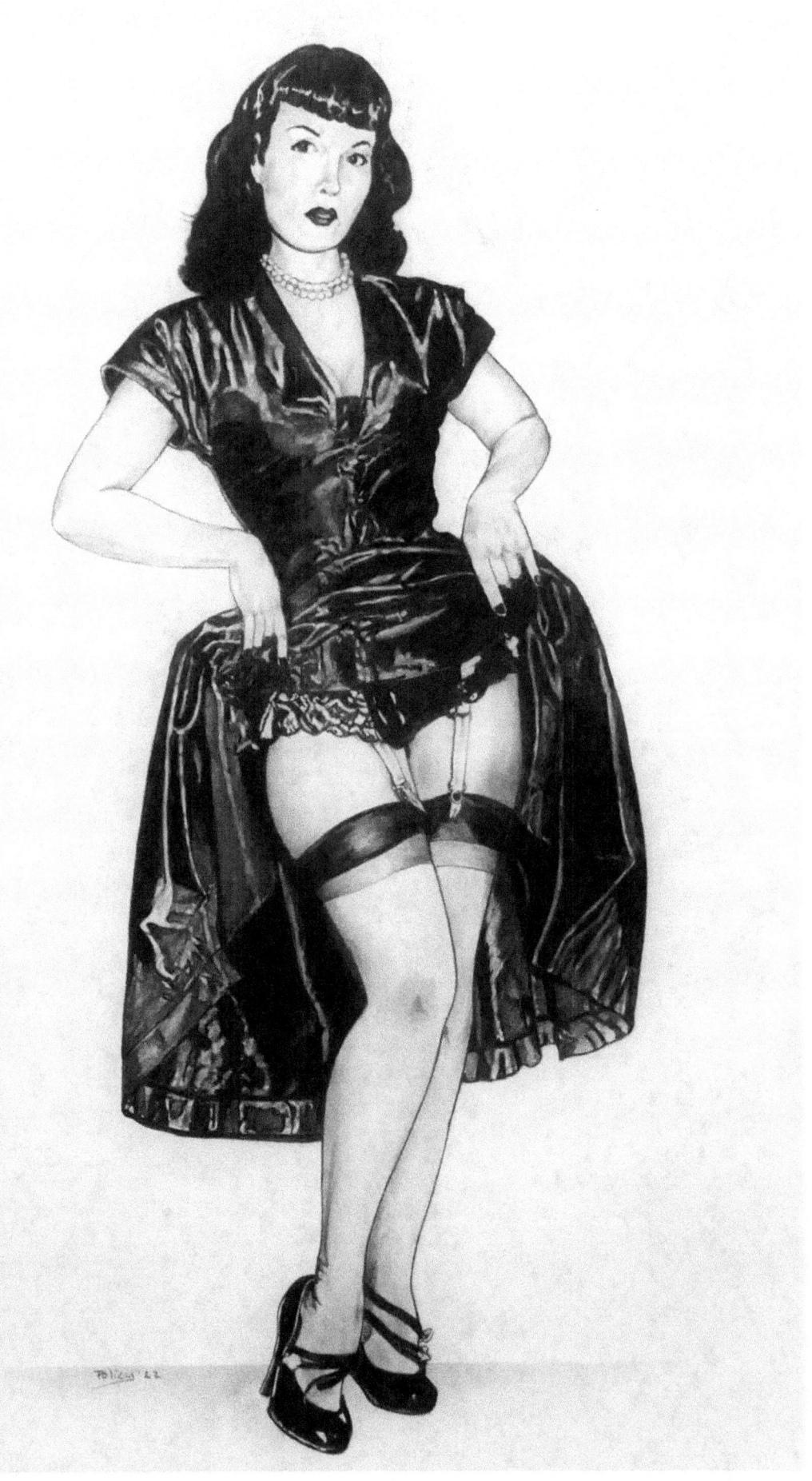

Like My New Shoes

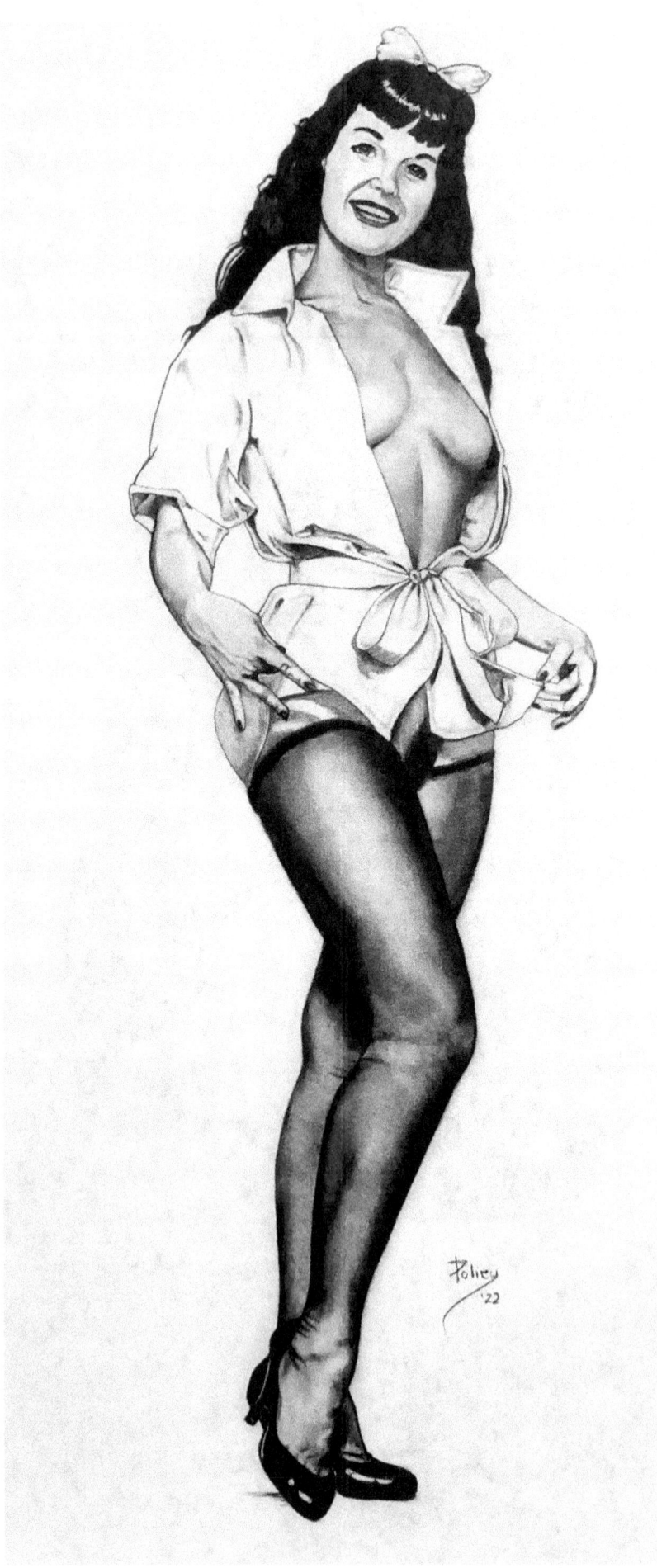

Barely Legal　　　　　　　　　　　　　　　　Next Page - Just a Thought

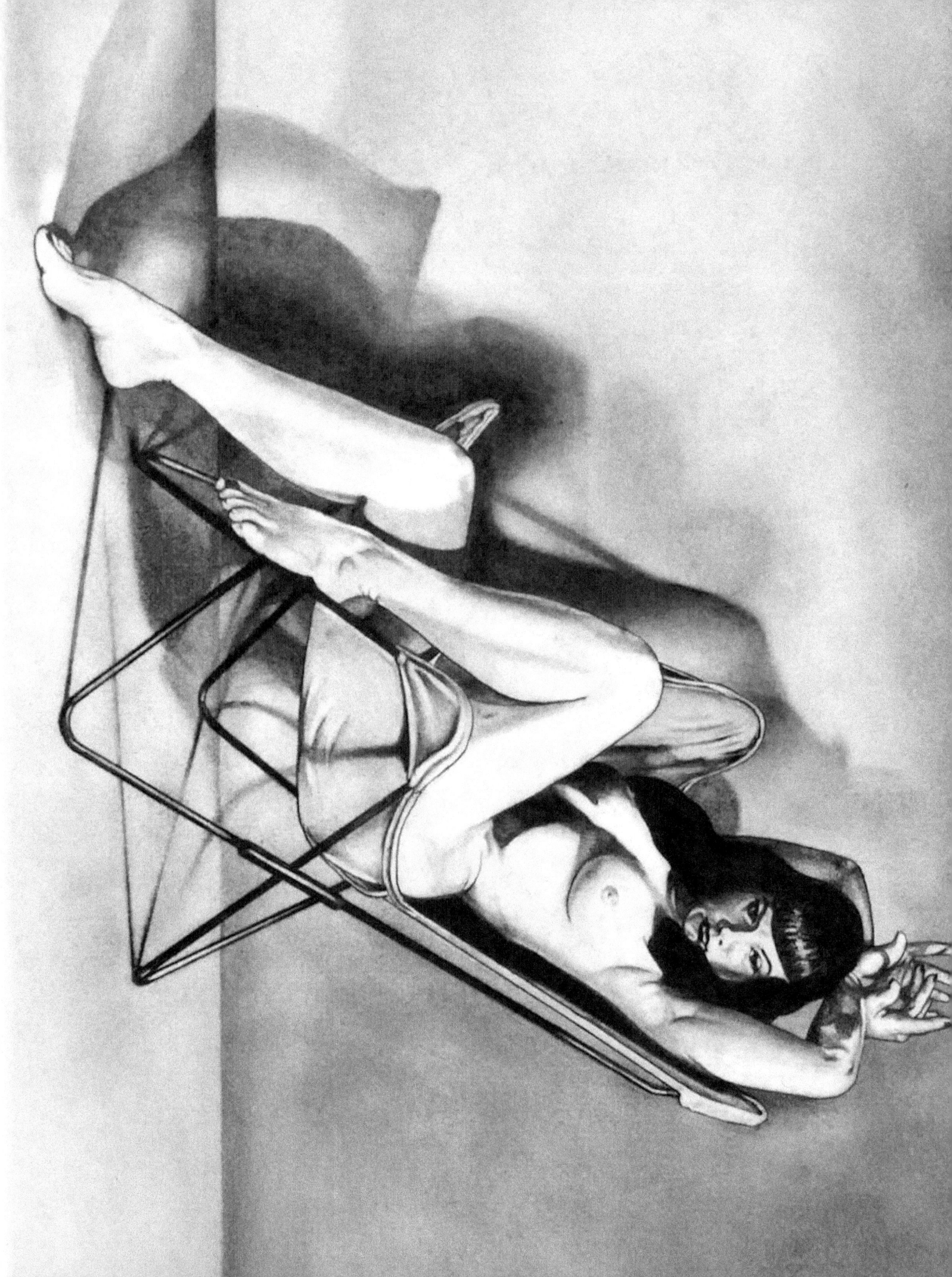

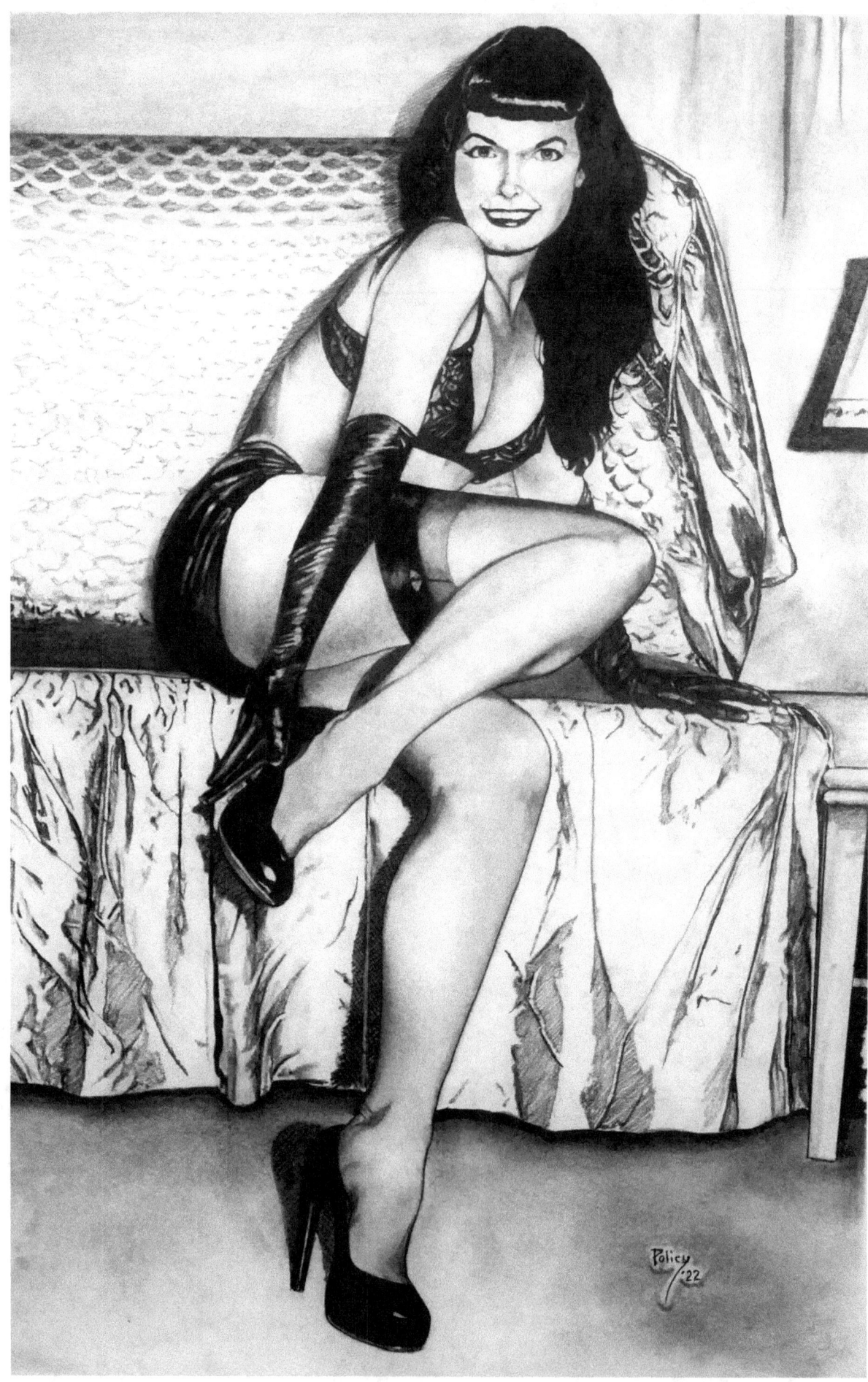

Couch Tomato

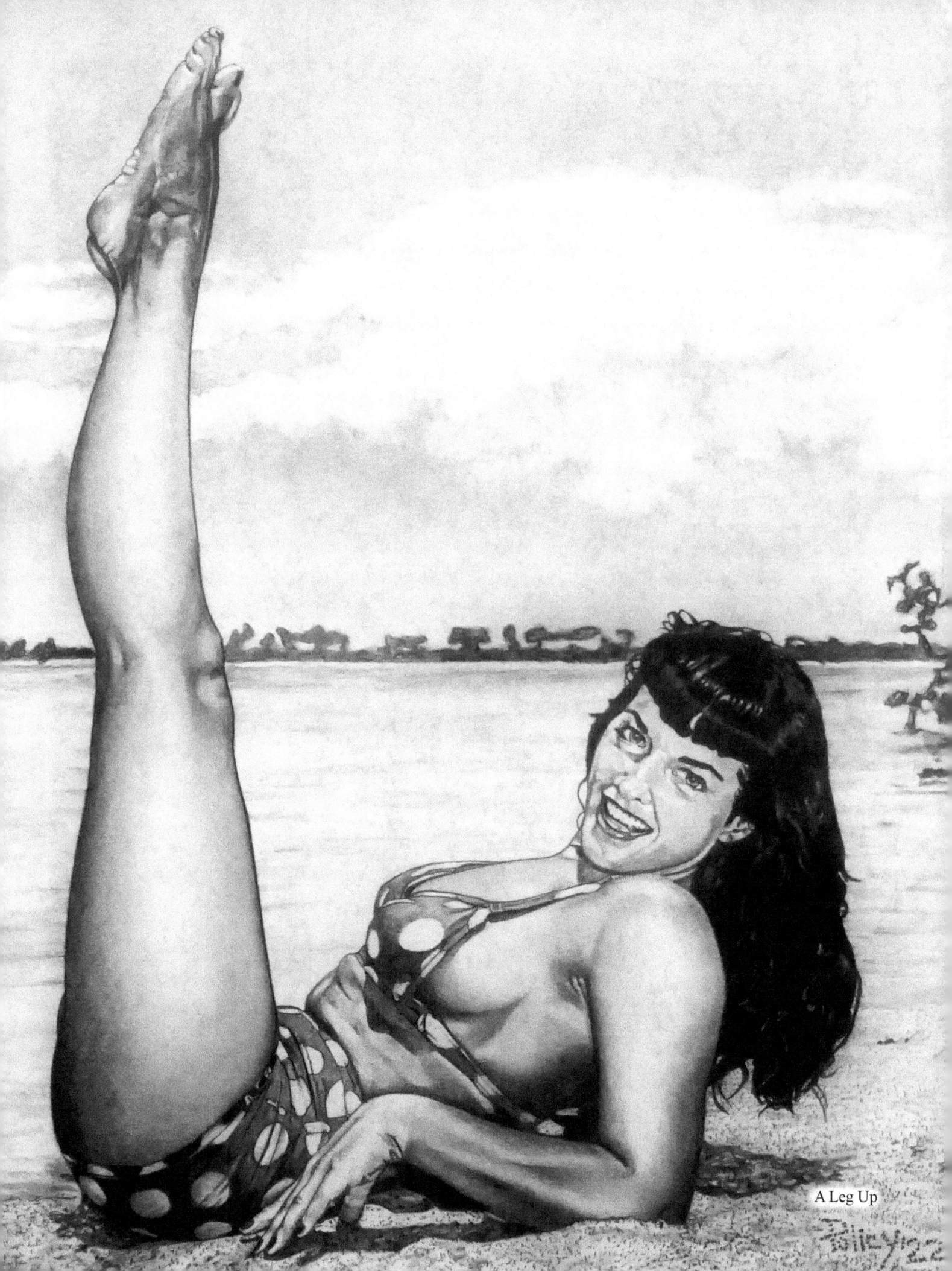
A Leg Up

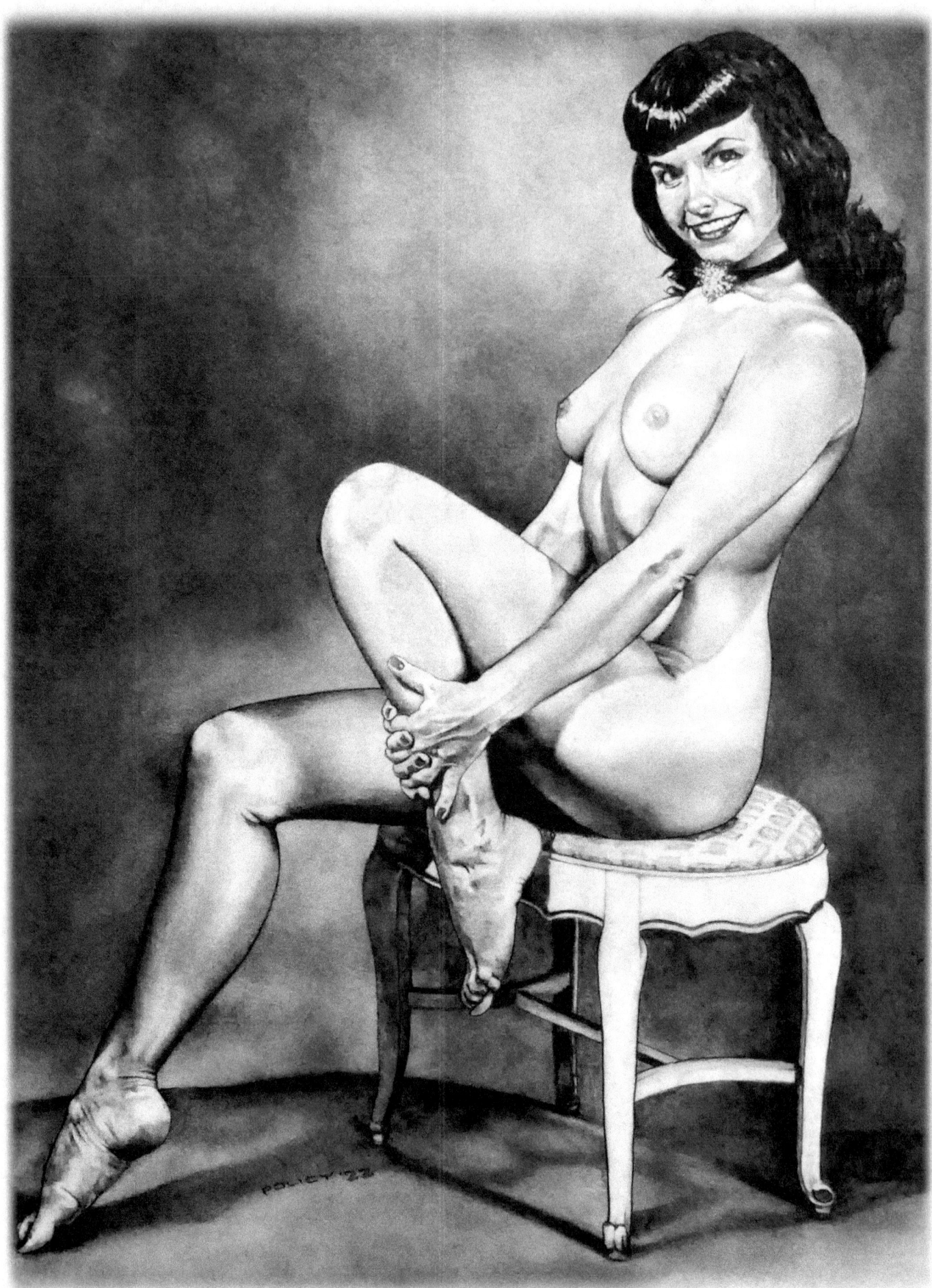

Background Check

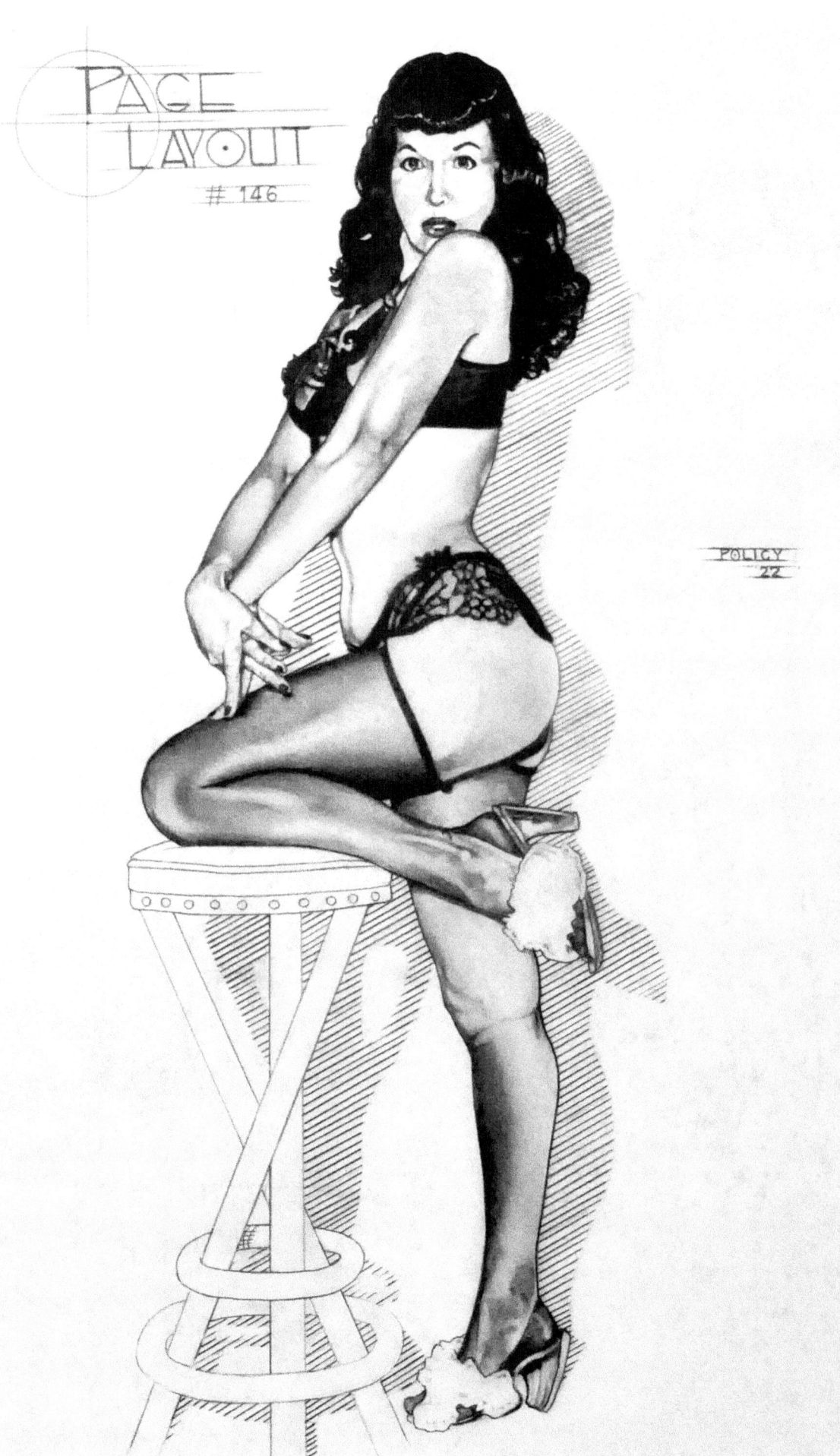

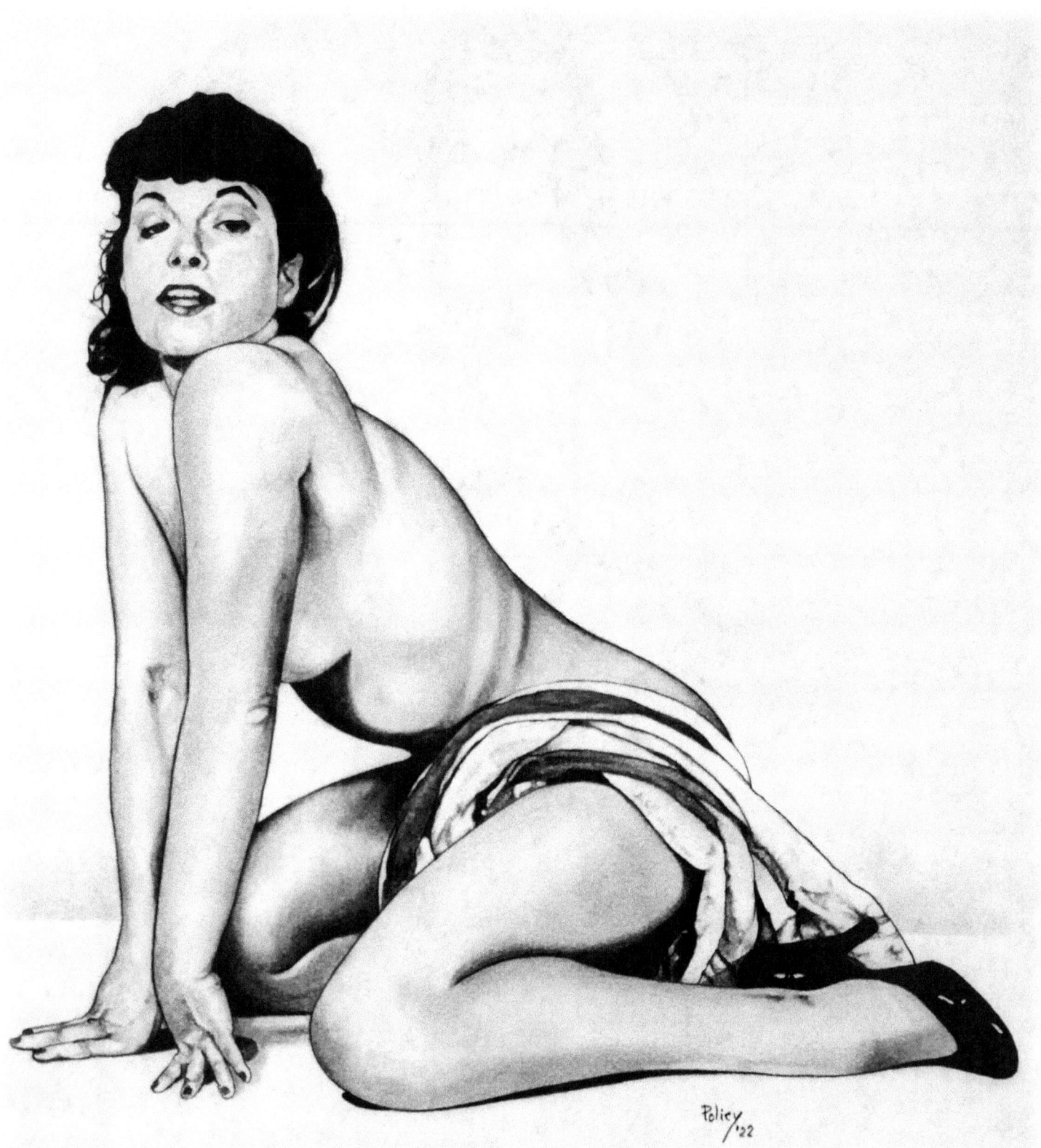

Towel Girl

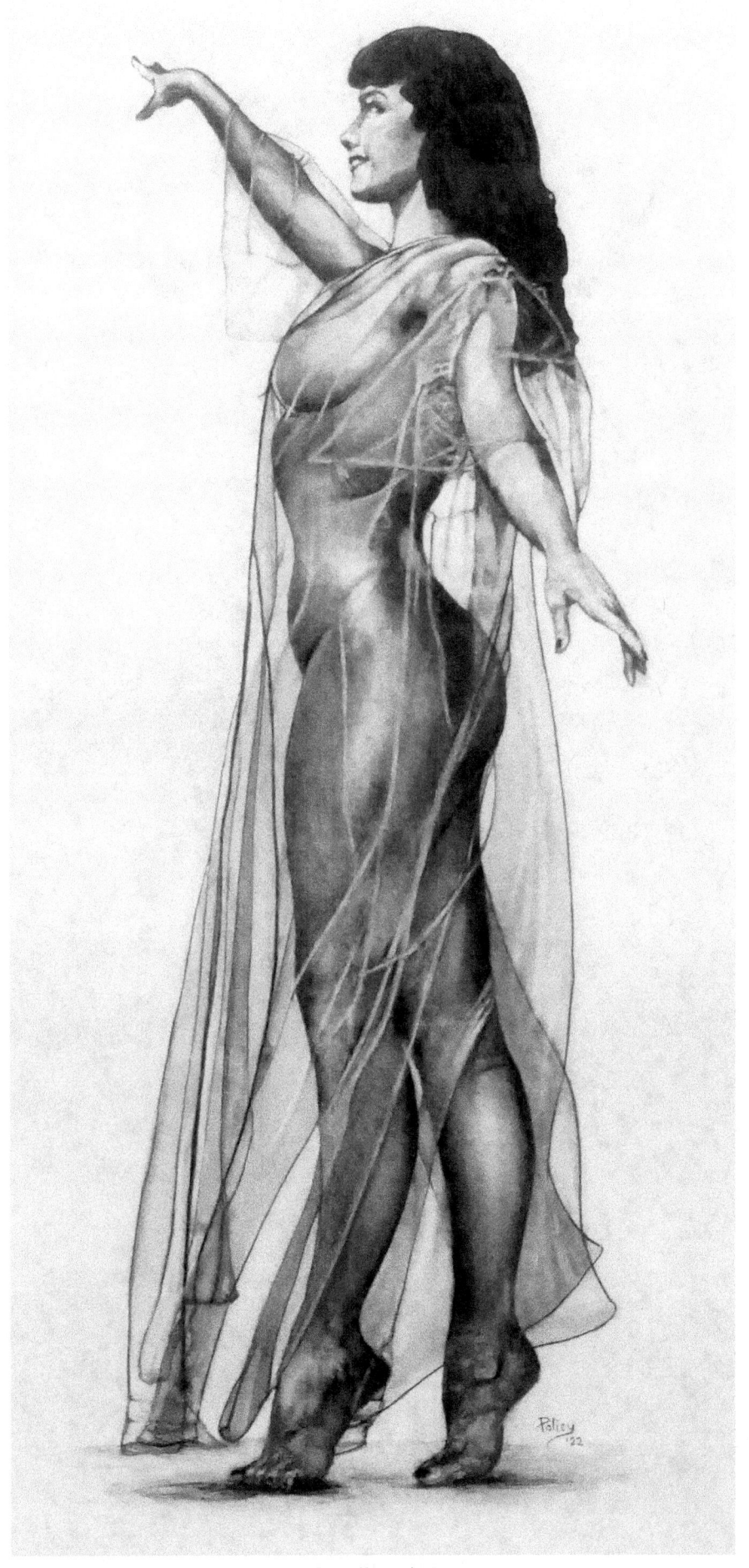

Standing Firm

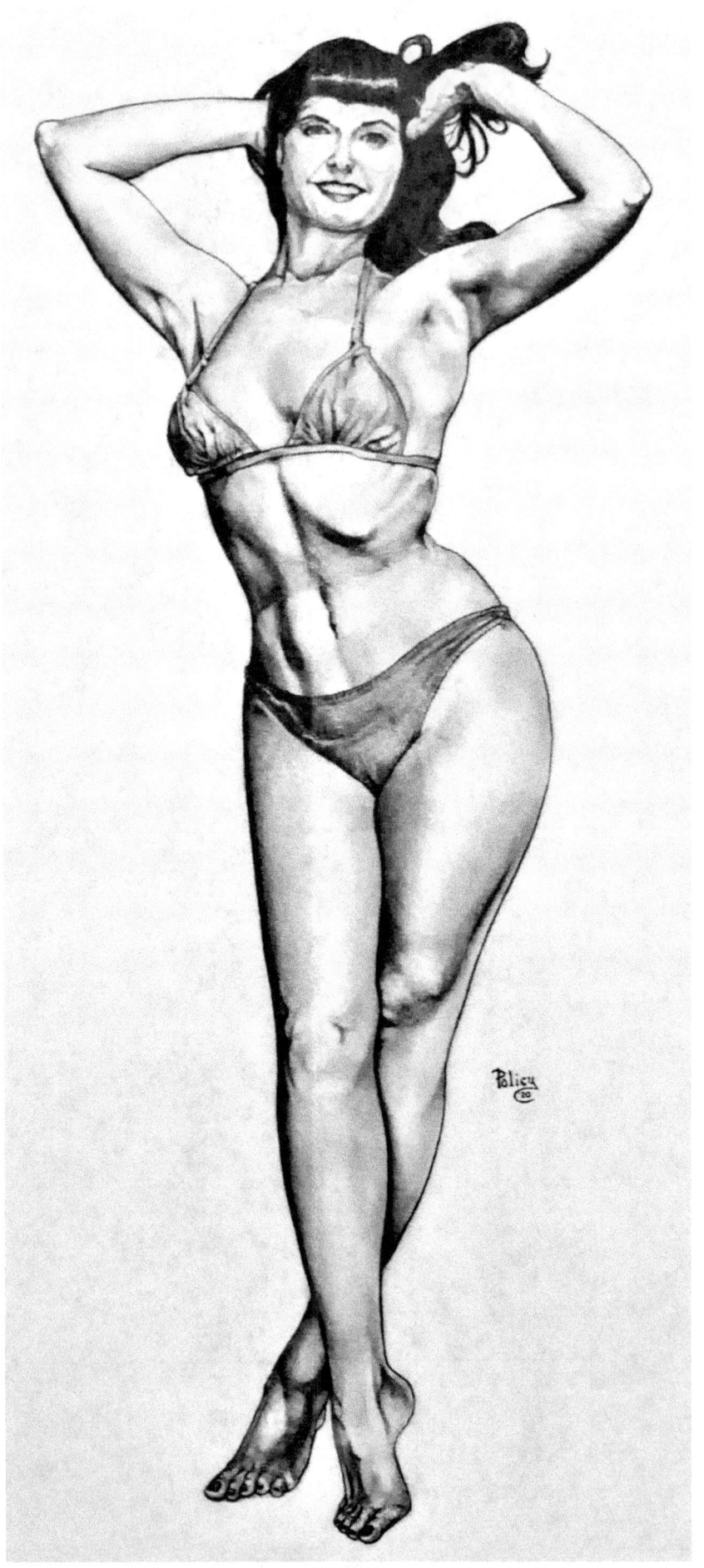

Just ... Out ... Standing

www.ingramcontent.com/pod-product-compliance
Lightning Source LLC
Chambersburg PA
CBHW062333220526
45469CB00008B/2697